EAT UP RAISE YOUR GAME

100 EASY, NUTRITIOUS RECIPES TO
HELP YOU PERFORM BETTER ON
EXERCISE DAYS AND REST DAYS

DANIEL DAVEY

GILL BOOKS

Gill Books
Hume Avenue
Park West
Dublin 12
www.gillbooks.ie
Gill Books is an imprint of M.H. Gill and Co.

© Daniel Davey 2019
978 0717184385

Designed by Fiachra McCarthy
Edited by Susan McKeever
Proofread by Jane Rogers
Indexed by Eileen O'Neill
Photography by Leo Byrne
Styling by Charlotte O'Connell
Printed by Printer Trento, Italy

This book is typeset in Quicksand

Information given in this book is not intended to be taken as a replacement for medical advice. Any person with a condition requiring medical attention should consult a qualified medical practitioner.

The paper used in this book comes from the wood pulp of managed forests. For every tree felled, at least one tree is planted, thereby renewing natural resources.

A CIP catalogue record for this book is available from the British Library.
5 4 3 2

For permission to reproduce photographs, the author and publisher gratefully acknowledge the following:

©INPHO/Donall Farmer: 7R; Sportsfile: 7C.

The author and publisher have made every effort to trace all copyright holders, but if any have been inadvertently overlooked we would be pleased to make the necessary arrangement at the first opportunity.

ACKNOWLEDGEMENTS

There are many people to whom I owe a big thank you for their help, support and feedback on the development of this book.

Thank you to my girlfriend Sandra who is the person I turn to every day for help and feedback on my meal ideas and recipes. She has done a huge amount of work proofreading and testing recipes and always provides endless support and love.

My sister Marianne who is one of my best friends and a fantastic cook. She has been there from the beginning when I burned the potatoes as a 10-year-old to now helping me with recipe ideas and giving me ongoing encouragement and ideas.

I would like to thank Gill Books and in particular Deirdre Nolan and all of the publishing team who believed in me and my concept. Without the support of Gill Books this book would not have been possible.

My mother Eileen and my father Peter who give me endless encouragement, the freedom to make mistakes, learn from them and who are always there when I need them.

To Brendan Egan, who has been my best friend and mentor in nutrition.

To my good friends Shane Kerins, Kenneth Kerins, Gary Kenny and Seán O'Brien, who helped to test my recipes and give me the help, encouragement and belief that this book could be achieved. As they say themselves, they are there to build me up but always keep me in line.

To Paul Mannion and Paul Flynn, who happily gave their time to be featured in this book and also give their insights on the importance of nutrition.

To Neil Irwin who assisted with the nutrition analysis and recipe information.

To Cathy Shivnan, Karen and Eoin McGowan, who kindly tested my recipes to make sure they worked!

CONTENTS

INTRODUCTION

There is one simple message I want to get across in this book: consistently eating good food can have extraordinary results. In my work with elite athletes, I've seen first-hand how the right diet can lead to trophies, personal bests and incredible physiques. But the good news is that it's not just in elite sport that tremendous results can be accomplished. Anyone can feel and perform better with the right food choices, appropriate exercise and good habits.

A healthy diet with appropriate energy and nutrients will make you feel energetic, positive, healthy, fit, strong and confident. In this book, I aim to help people experience these positive feelings every day by providing simple, delicious, easy-to-follow recipes that can be prepared quickly and shared with family and friends.

Along with giving the means to making and eating fantastic food, I want each recipe to be a learning experience, with key nutrition information delivered in a relaxed, accessible and practical manner.

WHERE IT ALL STARTED

I often get asked where my interest in food came from, and I've only recently realised what the answer to this question is. The experience of growing up on a small farm in Sligo in a family with strong food values had a huge impact on the way I view food. My mother is an excellent cook and through her, I developed a taste for meals created

"THE GOOD NEWS IS THAT IT'S NOT JUST IN ELITE SPORT THAT TREMENDOUS RESULTS CAN BE ACCOMPLISHED. **ANYONE CAN FEEL AND PERFORM BETTER WITH THE RIGHT FOOD.**"

from fresh vegetables and local meats. My father was a farmer but also worked in the local dairy, which produced fresh cream and butter. Being a farmer brings an appreciation for how valuable food is – his attitude was that food should not be wasted. He still talks about how he would steal the food off my plate if I complained about it, so I soon learned to eat what I was given.

As a young child, I stayed with both sets of grandparents when my parents went to work. My grandparents on both sides were dairy farmers but they also had gardens that supplied many of the vegetables, such as cabbages and carrots, for the kitchen. Fresh eggs were collected from the hen house each morning. In those environments, it was easy for me to see where food came from and why it was so important to eat nourishing food. Food meant nourishment, strength and growth and there was a clear link in my mind between eating the right foods and the potential to be a top-level Gaelic football player. My breakfast was always the same when I stayed with my grandparents: porridge or boiled eggs and homemade soda bread. Dinner was nearly always the same too: cabbage and bacon with carrots and potatoes freshly picked from the garden. Each of these meals was like a small celebration of what the farm produced. I distinctly remember what it felt like when my granddad told me what a great boy I was for eating all of my dinner – you would never dare leave your vegetables behind on your plate! I ate what my grandparents ate and they shaped my values on food. They also taught me to have huge respect for animals and to always show them care and attention.

HOME ON THE FARM

I still have a small sheep farm in Sligo where my dad tends to my sheep every day. Despite being based in Dublin, I try to get home as much as I can – there's nothing I enjoy more than tending the sheep and walking up the small mountain at the back of my house. I am very proud to be from a small farm in the West of Ireland.

We are incredibly fortunate in Ireland to have some of the world's best food and agricultural practices, which result in food of the highest quality. Buying local Irish produce has huge benefits, including environmental protection, sustainability and traceability. You might be surprised to hear that eating local produce also gives big nutritional benefits.

Jane, Sara, Rachel

Seán O'Brien and Daniel Davey

"WHEN PLAYING GAELIC FOOTBALL AT AN ELITE LEVEL, **I ALWAYS FOLLOWED NUTRITION BEST PRACTICE** AND I FOUND THAT MY OWN PERSONAL EXPERIENCE WAS VITAL WHEN EDUCATING"

SPORT AND PRACTICAL LEARNING

My next big influencing factor was sport. As a child all I wanted to be when I grew up was a Gaelic football player. I soon recognised that food was critical for growth, strength and performance. My nanny told me when I was growing up that if I wanted to be a really good football player I had to drink my milk, eat eggs for my breakfast and always have my vegetables at dinner. Thankfully, I did go on to play football through all the age grades with Sligo, then in Dublin with Ballyboden St Endas. When playing Gaelic football at an elite level, I always followed nutrition best practice and I found that my own personal experience was vital when educating others about how to achieve their performance potential or health goals.

UNDERSTANDING SCIENCE AND PERFORMANCE NUTRITION

It wasn't until I went to UCD to study agricultural science that I really began to understand science, food and nutrition. The coursework opened my eyes to how food impacts the body and my interest in nutrition intensified. The true meaning of farm to fork was something I began to fully appreciate.

My good friend Brendan Egan was doing his MSc in sports nutrition at Loughborough University at the same time, and through our many chats over the years he helped me to understand the broad concepts of that branch of nutrition. I decided that I wanted to go on to do sports nutrition and become a performance nutritionist.

Dublin GAA champs 2018

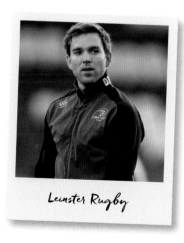

Leinster Rugby

Playing with Ballyboden St Endas

I graduated from Bristol University with an MSc in nutrition and physical activity and soon after got a job working with the London senior football team, which gave me invaluable problem-solving experience.

When I came back to Ireland I spent some time working with a sports nutrition company while also taking up my first significant nutrition role with the Dublin senior hurling team. It was in this environment that I fully began to appreciate how nutrition could impact overall performance. By using a combination of correct training and nutrition I could see the improvements in the team's body composition and overall fitness from week to week. The following season I got to work with the Dublin senior football team under Jim Gavin; then a month later I took the job of senior performance nutritionist with Leinster Rugby. Six years later I still combine the two roles in what I consider to be my dream job. I work with some of the best athletes in the country every day,

I help them to meet their nutrition goals and they challenge me to keep finding new ways to gain a performance edge for them in training and games. In both of these hugely successful teams, nutrition has been one of their key pillars of performance. The culture around nutrition is world class and the standards set by players continue to progress and evolve due to their winning mentality and professional attitude. I firmly believe that the nutritional know-how of both of these teams has played a major part in their success over the past six years.

"WE ARE **INCREDIBLY FORTUNATE IN IRELAND TO HAVE SOME OF THE WORLD'S BEST FOOD** AND AGRICULTURAL PRACTICES, WHICH RESULT IN FOOD OF THE HIGHEST QUALITY."

Dublin GAA champs 2018

Leinster Rugby,
European Champs 2018

Dublin GAA champs 2018

WHO IS THIS BOOK FOR?

Anyone who wants to raise their game! Whether you exercise recreationally or are a competitive athlete who's aiming to improve your performance, there is something in this book for you. You may just want a quick and tasty recipe, or you may be more focused on performance goals and post-workout recovery. Whatever your motivation, you'll appreciate the simplicity of my delicious recipes and enjoy learning about the health and performance benefits of each meal. I provide practical insights on how each recipe can be used on a daily basis through the nutrition information provided with each one. This will help people understand where different recipes fit into their nutrition goals.

The nutrition practices laid out in this book are evidence-based – most are driven by science, but sometimes it's just what has worked for me when preparing nutrition strategies for athletes and clients. I aim to be practical and to make the experience of consistently choosing the right foods highly enjoyable using easy-to-understand information and simple, tasty recipes. Knowing how to interpret the nutrition information on food labels, menus and of course in my recipes will make it easier for you to understand exactly what you are eating and stay on track for your personal needs.

> **MY PRIMARY FOCUS**
> when preparing meals is not simply to satisfy hunger but to achieve a real health and performance objective, such as:
>
> **1. MAINTAINING ENERGY LEVELS FOR DAILY ACTIVITIES.**
>
> **2. MEETING THE BODY'S NEEDS FOR MICRONUTRIENTS.**
>
> **3. PREPARATION FOR OR RECOVERY FROM EXERCISE.**

⏱ INVESTING TIME IN NUTRITION

Modern life is fast-paced and frantic. Time is always precious and the stress load from school, sport, college and work is growing all the time. This is often not a healthy combination as it can lead us to search for more convenient, processed food options, which only make stress levels worse. We need to make time for good nutrition habits – eating nutritious food with the right amount of energy. If you add to this a healthy lifestyle and frequent physical activity, wellbeing will follow. When possible we need to slow down and embrace cooking and food preparation as a positive activity in the home. Rather than looking at cooking as a chore or an inconvenience, try to shift your focus to look at it as one of the key activities that you use to invest in your health. There's no point in me giving you complex recipes with an ingredients list a mile long, as this will only create a barrier to you using them. Most of my meals can be prepared in 10 minutes and cooked in 20–30 minutes, which makes them perfect for busy lifestyles. One of the most common responses I've had to my recipes is, 'I never knew it would be so easy to make tasty meals!'

MINDFULNESS IN THE KITCHEN

The truth is that you will always have time to do things you prioritise. Poor management of your time results in bad decisions, and often the issue is inefficiency, not lack of time. If eating healthy food is a priority for you and you value your health the way you should, then you need to think ahead and schedule time to prepare your meals. If you don't do this, you may rush your food choices or pick something that is convenient or unhealthy. Enhancing your cooking skills and your understanding of what ingredients go well together can be an extremely rewarding experience, and the wonderful thing is that the journey never ends – your knowledge, skills and experience will continue to evolve.

BUILDING BETTER LIFESTYLE HABITS

The nutrition headlines that grab our attention often relate to quick fixes or short-term solutions for our health or appearance. We keep hearing about new, faster and easier ways to achieve our health goals, whether they are to lose fat, gain muscle or 'tone up'. The truth is, there's no quick fix to achieving your health and your fitness goals – you need to accept that it requires effort, planning and consistency. There is no such thing as the perfect diet or the perfect plan either. We are all different and we all struggle with different elements of our lifestyle. The key is to understand what suits you, and to stick to that plan without becoming distracted by what others are doing or trying something for a week then getting frustrated due to unrealistic expectations.

MY FOOD PHILOSOPHY

I have five strong beliefs about food
which I will share with you here.

1

I believe food should
be greatly valued, not
wasted, respected and
never taken for granted.

2

I believe in the ritual of
creating tasty and healthy
meals in a home each
evening that not only
provide nutrients to the
body but also bring families
and friends together.

3

I believe in learning key
cooking skills from your
family members, friends
and colleagues.

4

I believe that recipes and
meal ideas should be
shared and enjoyed.

5

My intention is not to debate the science of nutrition – there
are plenty of others who do that – but to translate this
science into the language of food and simple food choices.

10 SUGGESTIONS FOR LONG-LASTING AND SUSTAINABLE HABITS

1 LOG YOUR FOOD INTAKE FOR A WEEK IN A FOOD DIARY

By writing down everything you eat for one week you can see more clearly how much you are eating, what you are eating and when you are eating. This will give you a much better understanding of what areas you need to work on most. People are always surprised when they write down what they eat because it's easy to forget exactly what we eat from day to day. Keeping a food diary will help to identify if you are eating too many or too few calories. It will also highlight gaps in your diet and help you to plan meals that suit your schedule.

2 START BY FOCUSING ON ONE AREA TO IMPROVE

Rather than aiming to overhaul your diet, target one specific area for improvement first. This should be something that is most relevant to you and is the easiest thing to change, for example your breakfast. If you don't currently eat a healthy breakfast start by making sure you have a healthy breakfast each morning and build on that. As you become more consistent with that meal you can work on the next key area of your diet that needs improving.

3 SET REALISTIC TARGETS

Be realistic about what you want to achieve and give yourself plenty of time to achieve your goal. This could be related to losing or gaining weight or simply eating more fruit and vegetables. Judge your progress over a number of weeks rather than in days or just one week, as new habits take time to form. Take pride and belief in the small wins. For example, if you only eat two portions of vegetables a day at the moment, try to add one or two more portions of vegetables a day to your diet. Sticking to this consistently will make a big difference to overall nutrient intake and have positive impacts on your eating habits.

4 PLAN YOUR MEALS/RECIPES EVERY WEEK RATHER THAN CREATING A RIGID MEAL PLAN

People love the idea of meal plans and often think if they have the perfect meal plan they can follow it for their desired results. However, in reality, it never really turns out like that because people love variety and don't like to stick to the same food for long periods. A way around this is to construct a personal meal plan with different foods you enjoy for breakfast, snacks, lunch and dinner and swap in new ideas every week to create a healthy eating pattern.

5 MAKE SURE YOU HAVE HIGH-QUALITY COOKING UTENSILS

If you have poor-quality cooking utensils like blunt knives and pots that are constantly burning when you are cooking, you are more likely to think of cooking as a stressful chore. Sharp knives and a good set of pots and pans will ensure that your meal preparation and cooking run a lot smoother, making it a much more enjoyable experience to prepare your own meals.

6 ALWAYS HAVE HEALTHY FOOD IN THE FRIDGE AND GET-OUT-OF-JAIL FOOD IN THE FREEZER

All too often people go to their fridge or cupboard, hungry, and realise they have no healthy food to prepare. This leads to poor food choices such as instant noodles to curb their hunger! Make sure you have frozen fruits, frozen vegetables, yoghurt, milk, cottage cheese and some leftover or prepared meals in the fridge and freezer that you can use if you are too tired or short on time to cook. Cooking in bulk and preparing healthy snacks at the beginning of the week is another excellent way to help you stay on track with good food choices.

7 CREATE A SHOPPING LIST

It sounds so simple, and it is, but it's also very effective for keeping you focused on buying what you need rather than getting distracted by advertising and marketing claims when you are out shopping. Base your shopping list ingredients on your weekly meal plan and systematically move through the supermarket, getting what you need. Avoid the junk food aisles and the three-for-twos!

8 BUY DRY INGREDIENTS IN BULK

Make sure you never run out of essential dry ingredients again by keeping them topped up. Get some large glass or plastic airtight containers where you can store your dry grains, seeds and nuts (IKEA is a good place to shop for all kinds of containers). Non-perishable ingredients include oats, rice, mixed nuts, mixed seeds, lentils, milled flaxseeds, dark chocolate and your main spices. All you need to do is add some fresh

JUDGE YOUR PROGRESS OVER A NUMBER OF WEEKS RATHER THAN IN DAYS OR JUST ONE WEEK, AS NEW HABITS TAKE TIME TO FORM.

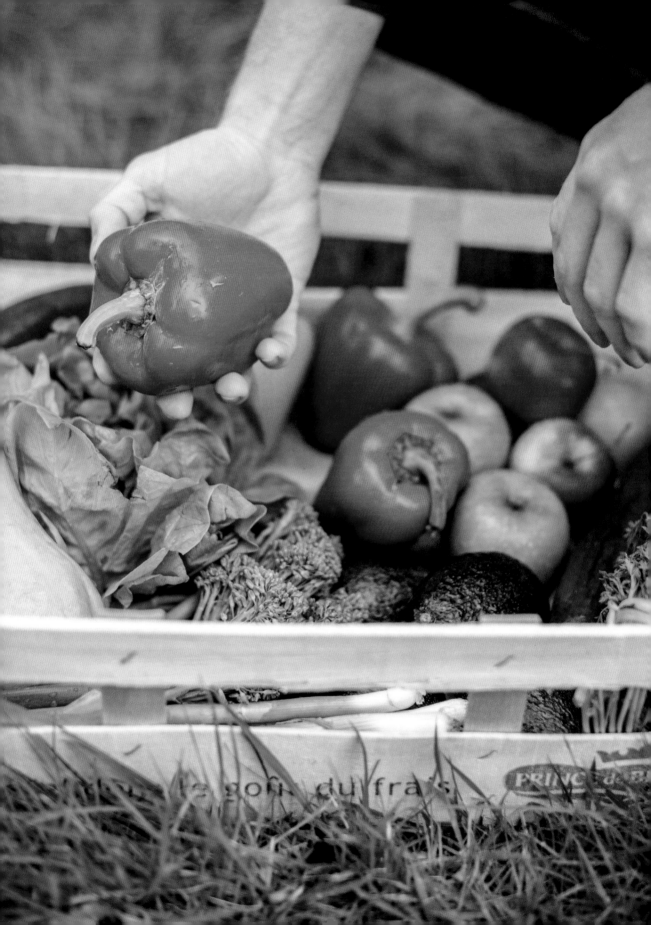

ingredients like vegetables, fruits, meat, fish or dairy and you're sorted to create main meals or snacks.

9 LEARN A NEW SKILL OR TECHNIQUE

Let's not over-complicate this one – it can be something really simple like learning how to peel vegetables properly, remove a stone from an avocado, cut up a pineapple or chop an onion. We can all improve one aspect of our cooking or baking skills, which will make life in the kitchen more efficient. If you are looking for demonstrations, there are loads of infographics and videos online that demonstrate various cooking skills. All of these new things help to build a better mindset towards good eating habits.

10 STAY POSITIVE AND BUILD MOMENTUM

We keep hearing about the importance of a positive mindset and how that can impact all aspects of our professional or personal lives. Remember that with any goal you are trying to achieve there will be ups and downs; it is rarely straightforward. When you do hit a sticky patch or make a few mistakes with your diet, stay positive and make sure that your next action is one that helps you focus and get back on track. This can be as easy as going for a walk, making a healthy meal or speaking to a friend who you know will give you some support. No matter how small the action, it can help you refocus and build up momentum to get back to consistent good habits.

👤 FOOD FOR THOUGHT

- When possible, eat fresh whole, natural foods.

- Check the origin – know where your food is produced.

- Use local ingredients where possible.

- Choose seasonal foods.

- Avoid foods that are processed and that contain added sugar, processed fats and other additives.

- Choose foods that are flavoured using natural flavour enhancers like honey, spices and herbs.

- Consider each meal for its nutritional value – not just energy, carbs, protein and fats but also micronutrients and antioxidants.

USING THIS BOOK

H ere's a breakdown of how to use this book: see the points below for a quick overview of the key concepts and how to plan your meals. If you're chomping at the bit to get cooking, you can then skip on to the recipes (page 71). Alternatively, if you want to understand performance nutrition principles in more detail, you can delve deeper into your energy needs, optimum recipe timings and individual macro requirements on page 22. How you use this book is entirely up to you.

A QUICK GUIDE

- You have different energy requirements each day depending on how much physical activity you are doing. Align your food choices to your level of physical activity on the day.

- Eat for your specific exercise needs – there are different nutrient and energy requirements depending on your age, gender, goal, sport or discipline.

- Choose recovery recipes or portions that are lower in energy and carbohydrates if you are only doing light activity or if you are doing an active recovery day that includes yoga or a light swim or cycle.

- Choose exercise recipes that are higher in carbohydrates if you are doing a significant level of physical activity or high-intensity exercise for a prolonged period (more than 60 minutes).

- Aim to consume a minimum of four portions of vegetables and three portions of fruit daily.

- Try to meet your need for fluids on a daily basis (at least 2.5 litres per day).

- Eat four to five protein foods during the day to support recovery, keep you satisfied and maintain muscle mass.

- Include fresh herbs, spices, seeds and berries into your daily diet – these are natural, nutrient-dense foods that support recovery and healing.

THE RECIPES IN THIS BOOK ARE
SPLIT INTO TWO MAIN CATEGORIES
BASED ON THE NUTRITION PROFILE
OF THE RECIPE.

Rest Day Recipe

Rest day recipes are nutritious
lower-carbohydrate recipes suitable
for less active and rest days.

Exercise Day Recipe

Exercise day recipes are nutritious
higher-carbohydrate recipes designed
to energise the body and support
recovery after exercise.

RAISE YOUR GAME

When it comes to food for health and exercise performance there is a hierarchy of daily goals a person should aim to achieve. This includes food quantity, macronutrients, the quality of the food you eat, meal timing and, finally, supplements. Prioritising these areas will help you stay focused on the specific components of nutrition that matter most. It will also help you identify the areas in your diet that can be developed and improved to help you achieve your health and performance goals.

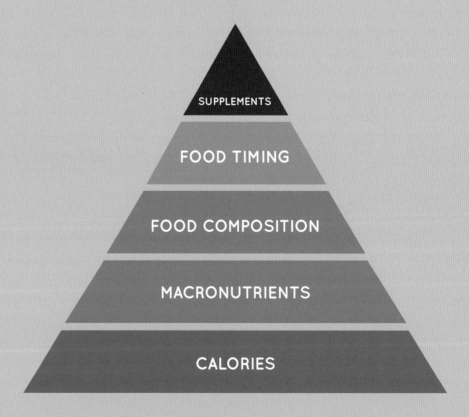

SUPPLEMENTS

FOOD TIMING

FOOD COMPOSITION

MACRONUTRIENTS

CALORIES

1
CALORIES

Meeting our appropriate level of energy is critical to be able to complete daily tasks. On the other hand, eating too many calories can lead to weight gain and its associated risk factors for lifestyle-related diseases.

2
MACRONUTRIENTS

In short, protein, carbohydrate and fat are our primary sources of energy from food. It's essential that we meet our personal needs for each one of these nutrients for health, energy, body composition goals and athletic performance.

3
FOOD COMPOSITION

This relates to the nutrient density of the foods we eat from day to day. Vitamins, minerals, fibre and antioxidants, found in abundance in vegetables, fruits, nuts and seeds, play a vital role in health, wellbeing and performance.

4
FOOD TIMING

Timing relates to when food is consumed. In general terms, this means at what point in the day; in a performance context it is specific to when food is consumed before or after exercise.

5
SUPPLEMENTS

These are often what people want to discuss first when considering their dietary goals, but this is the least important factor when it comes to the success of your diet. Having said that, in specific cases supplements can offer a valid solution for meeting the need for a particular nutrient.

1. CALORIES

For most people, it is not essential to count calories, assign points to food or avoid any food groups. Calories do of course matter and eating too many calories, even from unprocessed nutritious food, will lead to weight gain or fat storage. However, eating mostly fresh and unprocessed foods combined with regular physical activity will allow you to remain at a healthy body weight.

For athletes with a specific goal in mind, though, it's important to understand calories to achieve performance-related goals. The primary focus for an athlete's health, wellbeing and performance is to ensure they are consuming enough calories to offset the energy they're expending from physical activity. Have a look at the guidelines in this table that show energy intake based on levels of weight and physical activity.

ENERGY REQUIREMENTS FOR PHYSICAL ACTIVITY (CALORIE CALCULATOR)		
PHYSICAL ACTIVITY LEVEL	KCAL/KG/DAY	KCAL/DAY
General physical activity 30–40 minutes a day, three times a week	Normal diet, 25–35 calories per kg per day	1,800–2,400 (a)
Moderate levels of intense training two to three hours a day, five to six times a week (b)	50–80 calories per kg per day	2,500–8,000 (c)
High-volume intense training three to six hours a day, one to two sessions a day, five to six times a week (b)	50–80 calories per kg per day	2,500–8,000 (c)
a: Values estimated for a 50–80 kg individual b: Moderate levels of intense training use lower level of range; high-volume intense training uses upper level of range c: Values estimated for a 50–100 kg individual		

Taken from the International Society of Sports Nutrition position stands (ISSN) exercise and sport nutrition review: research and recommendations.

ESTIMATING CALORIE NEEDS

NAME	WEIGHT	GOAL	ACTIVITY	CALORIES
JANE	55kg	Health and weight maintenance	Desk job, mainly sedentary but does a yoga class one to two times per week	Daily calorie needs: **30kcal x 55kg = approx. 1,650kcal**
ANNE	65kg	Health and weight maintenance	One to two hours of intense physical activity 3 times per week	Daily calorie needs: **35kcal x 65kg = approx. 2,275kcal**
SARAH	55kg	High-performance athlete; health and weight maintenance	Two to three hours of high-intensity exercise >5 times per week	Daily calorie needs: **50kcal x 55kg = approx. 2,750kcal**
SHANE	70kg	Health and weight maintenance	Desk job, walks to and from work (30 minutes walking in total each day)	Daily calorie needs: **30kcal x 70kg = approx. 2,100kcal**
GARY	80kg	Health and weight maintenance	Desk job, does a 5km moderate intensity run after work one to three times per week	Daily calorie needs: **30kcal x 80kg = approx. 2,400kcal**
KENNETH	90kg	High-performance athlete; health and weight maintenance	One to three hours of moderate intensity exercise more than four times per week	Daily calorie needs: **40kcal x 90kg = approx. 3,600 kcal**

INDIVIDUAL CALORIE NEEDS

This is absolutely critical, folks, so please read carefully! The nutrition information for each recipe in this book is provided as a standard reference per serving based on someone eating approximately 1,800–2,500 calories per day. The aim of the recommendations is that you will comfortably be able to achieve your need for calories and macronutrients (the foods that make up the calories) by eating four to six meals each day. The reason these values have been chosen is that most of you will fall into these general calorie values, and if not, you can scale your number of meals up or down or adapt your portion sizes to meet your personal need for energy and macronutrients.

The table on the opposite page shows how you can estimate your calorie needs, based on six examples. The formula works like this: first, match your physical activity to the sample levels outlined in the table on page 24, then multiply your weight in kg by the value provided for your level of physical activity. It won't be 100 per cent accurate but it will give you a good guideline for your daily calorie needs.

Let's look at the first example to see how it works. Jane weighs 55kg, is mainly sedentary and spends most of her working day sitting at a desk. She does a yoga class as a form of low-level activity once or twice a week but not much more activity outside routine daily tasks. Jane wants to maintain her current weight and to better understand her daily energy needs. Based on this information, Jane chooses a lower calorie value level – 30kcal – as that matches her activity. She multiplies this by her weight in kg to get a value of 1,650kcal, which is an approximate measure of her calorie needs. By sticking to this number of calories, Jane should be able to maintain her current weight.

IMPROVING BODY COMPOSITION

Reducing body fat is probably one of the most talked about topics in the fitness industry. The actual concept of how to reduce fat mass is relatively straightforward: create a calorie deficit by expending more energy than you consume. However, in reality, fat loss is extremely complex due to the many physical, psychological, environmental and cultural factors involved. Achieving an improved body composition not only involves a clear nutrition plan, it needs a holistic approach, including an appropriate exercise plan, patience and discipline. This is not the focus of this book, but I will give a very short summary of the process of reducing body fat while maintaining optimum health and performance.

The aim for anyone with the goal of reducing body fat is to create a calorie deficit by making correct food choices in combination with training and lifestyle. However, you should also aim to improve your lean mass (muscle), or at the very minimum, maintain it. Muscle mass is critical for a healthy metabolism and a toned and fit physique. Often, people make the mistake of focusing purely on dropping body weight and this can be at the expense of lean mass.

The level of calorie restriction when aiming to reduce percentage of body fat depends on the person's level of fat mass. For example, if someone is aiming to reduce their fat mass by >5kg, then their deficit will be more severe compared to someone who is aiming to reduce fat mass by 2kg.

The target deficit for reducing fat mass can be 10% (conservative), 15% (moderate) and 20% (aggressive). If a person was to increase body mass in the form of lean mass the calculations would be exactly the same except you would add the percentage on to the daily calorie needs instead of taking them away.

There are approximately 7,700 calories in a kilo, and the goal is to achieve the required deficit over a set period of time. Here is an example of how a typical 80kg active male could achieve 1kg fat loss over three or four weeks. Gary is 80 kg, but wants to be 79kg. He exercises moderately 1–3 times a week but otherwise is relatively sedentary. His sleep patterns are consistent and is in good general health. Gary's level of physical activity is moderate so we will use the value of 30 (from page 26) multiplied by his body weight (80) to estimate his calorie needs. His calculations would look something like this.

MAINTENANCE: 80 x 30 = **2400 kcal**
15 % DEFICIT: **360 kcal**
TARGET CALORIES: 2400 – 360 = **2040 kcal**
TIME FRAME: 7700 ÷ 360 = **21 days**

2. MACRONUTRIENTS

As we learnt earlier, 'macronutrient' is the scientific name for the types of foods we eat – carbohydrates, protein and fats. Your main nutrition goal should be to establish a consistent and balanced eating pattern that provides your body with sufficient energy, a wide variety of micronutrients (vitamins and minerals), essential fats and antioxidants, while drinking enough fluids (p. 54). Eating a varied selection of vegetables, fruits, lean meats, fish, nuts and seeds while avoiding processed foods as much as possible will allow you to recover from your exercise sessions.

CARBOHYDRATES

There is no doubt that carbohydrate is the primary fuel required by those completing regular bouts of high-intensity exercise, and it is vital for optimal performance by athletes competing in high-volume intense exercise. In simple terms, high-intensity exercise means running, cycling, swimming at above

 FOOD FOR THOUGHT
....

The three critical factors for reducing body-fat while maintaining lean mass are:

1. Create a suitable calorie deficit
2. Achieve a minimum protein intake of 2g per kg body mass per day
3. Incorporate resistance exercise to maintain lean mass, strength and muscle function

For someone who exercises intensely on three or more days per week, here are the key principles to remember:

1

The majority of your carbohydrate needs should be met on training days.

2

Aim to eat a wide variety of fresh fruits and vegetables to meet your nutrient requirements.

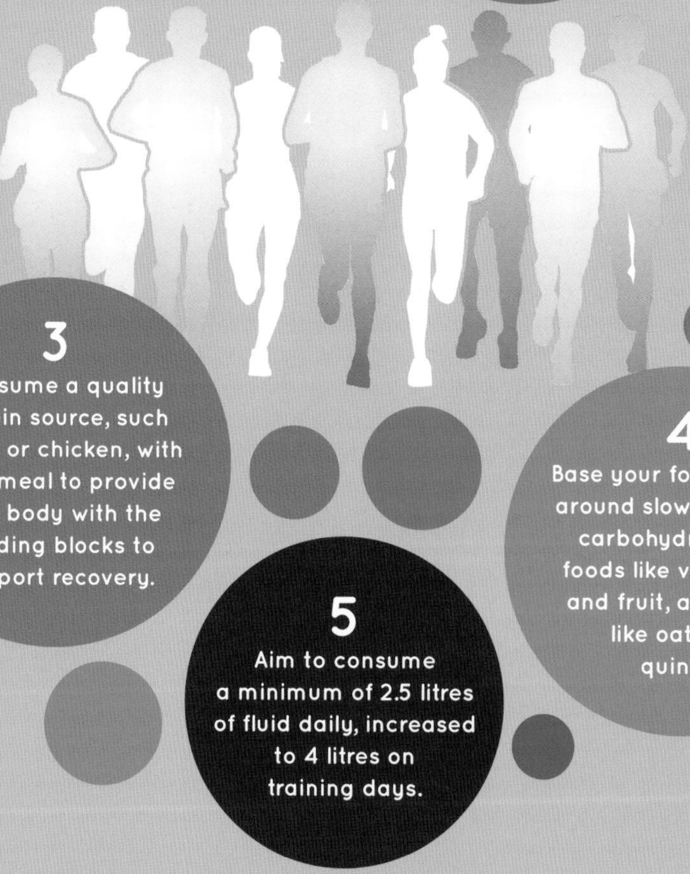

3

Consume a quality protein source, such as fish or chicken, with each meal to provide your body with the building blocks to support recovery.

4

Base your food choices around slow-digesting carbohydrate-rich foods like vegetables and fruit, and grains like oats and quinoa.

5

Aim to consume a minimum of 2.5 litres of fluid daily, increased to 4 litres on training days.

70 per cent of total exercise capacity. This means your heart rate is at 70 per cent of your maximum heart rate, which can be calculated by subtracting your age from 220. Another way to judge it is by using the 'talk test' – you should not be to talk consistently or say more then a few words at this intensity.

Anyone who does regular physical activity has no reason to avoid carbohydrate foods. Fat is the primary fuel used during slow or moderate intensities of exercise such as walking, slow jogging, light-intensity cycling or swimming. At this pace, the body's energy system relies much more on our fat stores rather than circulating sugar and glycogen (the body's carbohydrate stores).

Recreational athletes need considerably less carbohydrate than those completing high volumes of high-intensity running. In fact, people who are mainly recreationally active may benefit more from mainly eating carbohydrate-rich foods only on exercise days. This allows the body to use its fat

 FOOD FOR THOUGHT

- Carbohydrate is the primary fuel required by those completing regular bouts of high-intensity exercise.
- Your need for carbohydrate is dependent on your level of physical activity.
- Your need for carbohydrate is lower on days when you are less active and higher on days when you are more active.

stores as a source of energy, and also allows for more efficient use of carbohydrate when it is consumed around training. That is not to say that carbohydrate is not necessary for performance. It's better to think of it from the perspective of fuelling for the work required. A person doing manual labour, like block-laying for example, requires much more energy than someone sitting at a desk all day. In other words, eat more carbs on days when you are completing moderate or

CARBOHYDRATE GUIDE BY BODY WEIGHT	
ACTIVITY	**GRAMS**
Light physical activity (walking, cycling, yoga, etc.)	2–3g per kg
Light to moderate-intensity exercise (45–60 minutes)	3–5g per kg
High-intensity endurance exercise (one to three hours)	6–10g per kg
Extreme high-intensity and high-volume exercise (three to five hours); if you are competing in an event like the Tour de France	10–12g per kg

Information adapted from American College of Sports Medicine Joint Position Statement for Nutrition and Athletic Performance.

high-intensity exercise compared to days when you are mainly inactive.

When training regularly, you should consume foods that provide the body with a steady supply of energy. Carbohydrate needs can easily be met from eating whole foods like oats, root vegetables and fruits. So, on exercise days, you could eat porridge for breakfast, fruit and nuts for snacks and some sweet potato or quinoa for lunch and dinner. You should eat your last meal at least two to three hours before you train. The quantity of these foods does not have to be large as small portions will often more than

adequately meet your energy needs for training or a workout. After exercise, a small snack, fruit smoothie or a balanced meal with vegetables and lean meat will promote optimum recovery.

PROTEIN

Protein is the primary nutrient that supports growth and repair in the body. It's what makes up muscle tissue; it also provides a source of energy for cells of the immune system. Active people should aim to consume 1.7–2.0g of protein per kg of body mass per day depending on their health or performance goal. The reason why athletes take protein (in whatever form) after exercise is to promote recovery by helping to repair damaged muscle fibres, but protein is also involved in countless other functions such as reducing muscle protein breakdown and facilitating hormone production and immune support, all vital for recovery. For optimum protein distribution across the day, it is generally recommended that people aim for 20–40g of protein per meal for an even distribution of their protein intake. In practical food terms, this means consuming four meals (three mains and one snack) containing a protein source like mixed grains, milk, yogurt or eggs for breakfast, and pulses, lentils, meat or fish, for lunch and dinner. The guideline for protein intake after intense performance is 0.3–0.5 grams per kg body mass, which is 24–40g of protein for the average 80kg male or 20–32g for a 65kg female, but more for larger athletes. You can easily meet protein requirements post-workout by eating whole

🗣 FOOD FOR THOUGHT

■ Protein is an essential building block for muscle tissue and is critical for growth and repair in the body.

■ If you're active you should aim to consume 1.7–2.0g of protein per kg of body mass per day, depending on your health or performance goal.

■ You can easily meet your daily protein requirements by eating a balanced diet that includes protein-rich foods.

■ Protein intake should be spread throughout the day and not just eaten at lunch and dinner. This will support recovery from training, maintain lean mass and keep energy levels stable.

OILY FISH

Marine plants and animals are the best sources of omega-3 fats in the food chain. The omega-3 fats in fish such as salmon and mackerel are 'bioavailable', which means that the body can use them for many beneficial functions, including brain activity and cardiovascular health. Aim to consume at least three servings of oily fish per week (see page 60 for information on taking fish oil as a supplement).

FLAXSEEDS/ FLAXSEED OIL

Whole or milled flaxseeds and flaxseed oil are a rich source of omega-3 – add to smoothies, porridge or yoghurt or include them in homemade snack bars and pancakes.

FOOD SOURCES OF HEALTHY FATS

NUTS

Pecans, macadamia nuts and especially walnuts are packed with omega 3-fats. Nuts are an excellent snack between main meals or you can add them to salads and main dishes for texture and flavour. Be careful to choose raw or roasted nuts – sugar- and chocolate-covered nuts are not a healthy choice!

OMEGA-3- ENRICHED EGGS

Look out for omega-3-enriched eggs in the supermarket – these are produced by pasture-fed, free-range chickens that have been fed an omega-3-rich diet. The eggs from these chickens contain extra-high levels of omega-3 fats so switching to these is a great way to up your intake of this essential fat.

foods such as lean meats and fish in the recovery meal, but some people do struggle to eat dense food after exercising due to a sensitive stomach or lack of appetite. In this case, a liquid recovery meal like a recovery drink or whey protein fruit-based smoothie is perfect to provide these essential nutrients in a more tolerable form.

FATS

Fats are vital for cardiovascular health, brain function, hormone production, immune function and replenishment of fat stores within the muscles. Eating the right kinds of fats is important for everyone but especially for people who exercise regularly at a high intensity. Fat intake should range from 25 to 35 per cent of total energy intake.

There are two essential fats required by the human body:

- **Omega-3 alpha-linolenic acid**
- **Omega-6 linoleic acid**

These are both polyunsaturated (healthy) fats. They cannot be produced (synthesised) by bodily processes, so you need to include them in your diet – hence the term 'essential'. Eating healthy sources of fat will not only provide essential fatty acids but also essential fat-soluble vitamins including vitamins A, D, E and K. Omega-3 fatty acids are suggested to play a key role in brain development, neurological and cardiovascular health, and may have beneficial effects on body composition.

In terms of total energy intake, healthy fats should make up a minimum of 25 per cent of your total calorie intake. This intake can be achieved quite easily by consuming the foods listed on the previous page with your main meals and snacks, and staying away as much as possible from processed foods. When you combine these foods with a high-quality fish oil supplement you can rest assured that your body is getting all the daily essential fats it needs.

FIBRE

Fibre! Most health-conscious people are aware of its importance for health and good digestion, but few people know just how vital it is and why. Dietary fibre, which is also commonly known as roughage, is the part of

TWO MAIN TYPES OF FIBRE

SOLUBLE FIBRE: As the name suggests, this fibre is soluble in water, but it expands and forms a gel-like substance when mixed with water. This process slows the movement of food through your digestive system, giving you a feeling of fullness and by slowing digestion it often allows for a steady, rather than rapid, rise in blood sugar levels after a meal.

INSOLUBLE FIBRE: Because it is not water-soluble, this type of fibre assists with the transit of food and waste material through your digestive system. Insoluble fibre helps hydrate and move waste through the intestines and also plays an important role in regulating pH (acidity level).

DAILY FIBRE

The most recent recommended daily allowance (RDA) for fibre for both children and adults are 14g/1,000kcal, or a minimum of 25g daily for women and approximately 30–40g for men. Although this doesn't sound like much, many people are not meeting this basic daily requirement, despite knowing how important it is for good health. Recent research on fibre intakes in the Irish population found that three out of four adults are not meeting the RDA for fibre.

BENEFITS OF A FIBRE-RICH DIET:

1. It lowers the risks of developing coronary heart disease, stroke, hypertension, diabetes, obesity and certain gastrointestinal diseases.
2. It is a key element for anyone looking to reduce body fat and to improve body composition – generally speaking, eating fibre-rich foods usually means you feel fuller for longer.
3. High-fibre foods, such as broccoli, green beans, lentils and oatmeal, are usually low in calories.
4. It lowers blood pressure and serum cholesterol levels as well as helping to control blood sugar levels.

The best sources of fibre are whole, unprocessed foods like fruit, whole vegetables, legumes, nuts and seeds. Rolled or steel-cut oats, buckwheat and quinoa are examples of excellent high-fibre grain varieties.

A WORD OF WARNING:

There are some occasions when fibre intake should be kept low, such as in the hours before performing high-intensity exercise like running. High-fibre foods can cause excess gas and bloating during exercise, so make sure you only eat low-fibre foods like white rice or potato and noodles in the three to six hours before your workout.

food that we eat (mainly from plants) that cannot be digested or absorbed by the body. Technically it is a type of carbohydrate, but when we eat fibre it passes through our body undigested, and thereby supports the transit of food through the gut and the removal of waste material.

Long ago, fibre was not an issue. People ate large amounts of fresh vegetables and fruits which meant that their daily fibre intake was more than sufficient for digestive health, and not really a general health concern. Nowadays fibre is an issue – mainly because the 'Western' diet contains so many highly processed calorie-dense foods. Processing removes much of the fibre in foods, and unfortunately, eating processed food usually means that you eat more without really feeling that full! To make things worse, people are also eating fewer fresh, whole vegetables and fruits, which are rich in both insoluble and soluble fibre. The consequence of this is that food companies are now adding fibrous ingredients back into foods, creating a surge in foods with 'added grain' or 'whole grain' varieties of foods such as breads, crisps, flours and similar – although it is questionable as to whether this makes these foods any healthier.

3. FOOD COMPOSITION

A large number of factors influence the food choices we make and the dietary practice we decide to implement. What we can all agree on in the nutrition field is that plants in the form of vegetables, fruits, nuts, seeds and whole grains should provide the greatest proportion of energy in our diet. A simple example of this is outlined in the pyramid, which includes six portions of fruit and vegetables, protein foods like eggs, meat, fish, poultry, and whole grains like quinoa and oats. The amount of these foods can easily be matched to your energy and macronutrient needs.

Protein

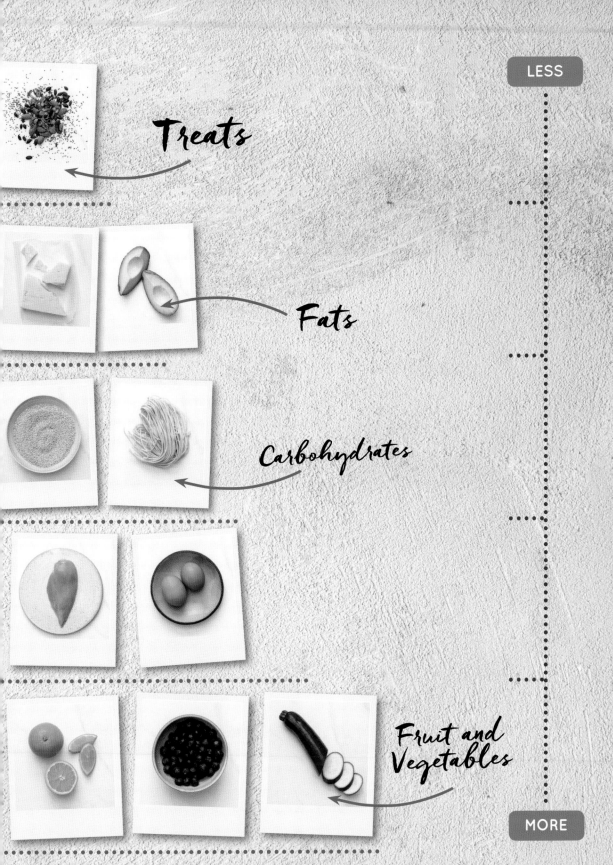

LESS

Treats

Fats

Carbohydrates

Fruit and
Vegetables

MORE

PORTION SIZES

Portion size is something that people often find difficult to understand. Trying to read labels and track the number of calories and macronutrients in a meal can be confusing due to the huge variety of ways in which nutrition information is displayed on labels and food products. There are countless nutrition trackers online or in app form but for those who still find it difficult to estimate ideal portion size, there's a simple method that you can use with no technology whatsoever – all you need is your hand! Here's how the 'hand portion guide' works:

Your fist equals a portion (80g) of vegetables or fruit.

Your palm equals a portion (100g) of protein from poultry, meat or fish.

A cupped palm equals a portion of nuts or a carbohydrate portion from rice or pasta.

Your thumb equals a portion of fats like cheese or nut butter.

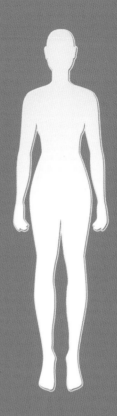

MEN

Will normally require **two palm-sized portions** of protein at main meals, 40-60g.

Will normally require **two fists of vegetables** at main meals.

Will normally require **two palmfuls of carbohydrate** with main meals, 40-60g.

Will normally require **one to two thumbs of healthy fats**, 15-25g.

WOMEN

Will normally require **one to one and a half palm-sized portions of protein** at main meals, 20-40g.

Will normally require **one fist-sized portion of vegetables** at main meals.

Will normally require **one palmful of carbohydrate** with main meals, 30-40g.

Will normally require **one to one and a half thumbs of healthy fats**, 10-15g.

PLANTS IN FOCUS

Ask any 10-year-old how many pieces of fruit and vegetables they should eat every day, and they'll give a quick and accurate response of five a day! 'At least' five portions of fruit and vegetables per day is the quantity recommended by the World Health Organisation (WHO). One portion of fruit and vegetables = 80g, which brings recommended daily consumption to a total of 400g. What does this mean in real food terms? It could be one medium-sized apple, one medium-sized orange and three cups each of broccoli, butternut squash and bell peppers. Even though most people are aware of this recommendation, figures show that on average Irish people are not meeting these guidelines. The National Adult Nutrition Survey (NANS 2011) report revealed that the average intake of fruit and vegetables in 18–64-year-old Irish adults was just 192g per day; only 9 per cent of this age group met the WHO guideline.

Interestingly, in other nations including France, Canada and Denmark, people are recommended to consume a minimum of six, but aim for ten, portions of fruit and vegetables daily. Our European neighbours in Spain (605g per day), Italy (479g per day) and France (467g per day) are clearly taking heed of the guideline, while in Japan, the recommended intake of fruit and vegetables is 17 portions per day!

SO, HOW MUCH FRUIT AND VEGETABLES SHOULD WE EAT DAILY?

The aim should be to eat some form of fruit or vegetables with every meal or snack. That might sound extreme, but this might add up to just seven to nine portions of fruit and vegetables a day. Remember, the five-a-day rule should be considered the bare minimum. I think people often forget that the rule says at least five a day, not only five a day!

This is something that I take into consideration when developing my main meal recipes. I always ask myself, can I make this recipe more nutritious by adding more vegetables? Smoothies, soups and stir-fries are great for people who find it challenging to eat enough fruit or vegetables.

Fruit and vegetables are not only packed with nutrients that keep the body healthy, they also provide a sustained supply of energy by steadying our blood sugar levels, support good bowel function through the presence of fibre, and play a key role in immune function. Substantial evidence now supports the following benefits from eating a minimum of 400g (5 x 80g portions) or more of fruit and particularly vegetables:

- **Reduced risk of disease such as cancer and cardiovascular disease**
- **Improved body composition**
- **Better gut health**
- **Enhanced energy levels**
- **Stronger immunity**
- **Enhanced digestion**

VEGETARIAN AND VEGAN DIETS

Beliefs about animal rights and environmental issues, combined with perceived health benefits of a plant-based diet, have recently caused a surge in people turning vegetarian or vegan. There is no question that aspects of a vegetarian diet have benefits, mainly because of a greater intake of vegetables and fruits, which are rich sources of fibre, vitamins, minerals, antioxidants and health-promoting nutrients. However, because vegetarians and vegans avoid animal products, which are the richest source of

protein in an omnivorous diet, they must make a conscious effort to eat enough protein-rich plant-based foods to meet their daily protein requirements. This is especially true for people undertaking intense exercise because that increases the body's daily protein needs. Instead of presenting you with the pros and cons of a vegetarian or vegan diet, I'm going to provide some practical suggestions on how vegetarians, or anyone for that matter, can meet their daily requirement for protein from suitable plant sources. It's entirely achievable but does require a bit more planning and preparation of meals, instead of just reaching for a chicken breast or salmon darne.

The good news is that you can combine two plant sources of protein to create a meal that provides all the essential amino acids your body needs. Some of the best foods to combine to provide a complete amino acid profile are:

- Chickpeas, beans and quinoa
- Mixed beans and brown rice
- Hemp, chia and pumpkin seeds with oats
- Mixed nuts and seeds with beans in a fresh salad
- Oatmeal muesli with mixed nuts and seeds
- Buckwheat with beans and fresh green vegetables

Vegetarian recipes in this book are marked with

Below is a short list of protein-rich plant-based foods which provide a good source of protein and can be incorporated into a vegan or vegetarian diet to help you hit your protein targets.

TOFU

Tofu is a highly versatile and nutritious food that is made from curdling soy milk (from soybeans) and pressing it into small blocks. Tofu has 76 calories, 4g of fat, 2g of carbohydrate and 8g of protein per 100g. Just to give you an idea of how much you'd need to eat for a good protein boost, one chicken breast = about 400g of tofu.

QUINOA

Most grains contain a small amount of protein, but quinoa (technically a seed) is unique in that it contains more than 9g per 200g serving. Quinoa contains all nine of the essential amino acids that need to be taken in the diet. Added to that it's gluten free, which makes it a great option for those who can't eat gluten.

SHELLED HEMP SEEDS AND HEMP PROTEIN

Hemp is one of the very few plant proteins that supply you with all essential amino acids. Hemp seeds are great in muesli or added to homemade bread or simple snack bars. You can also take it in protein powder form, but I have to admit it tastes a bit like wet sand!

CHIA SEEDS

Tiny, blackish chia seeds come from a flowering plant in the mint family that is native to Mexico and Guatemala. Chia seeds were a valuable food crop for the Aztecs and can make a positive contribution to the modern diet because they are a source of omega-3 fats as well as a good source of protein. Chia seeds are tasty and packed with fibre. Add them to homemade bars, smoothies and muesli mixes or include them when cooking your porridge.

LENTILS

Whether they are brown, green, red, yellow or black, lentils (a type of pulse) are a great source of protein. Just 200g

COMPLETE PROTEIN

A complete protein (mostly from animal sources) contains all of the essential amino acids, or protein building blocks, that the body needs.

INCOMPLETE PROTEIN

An incomplete protein (often from plant sources) is missing one or more of these essential amino acids.

of cooked of lentils contains 18g of protein, which can really boost your protein intake in any main meal. Use them in curries, soups or salads.

GREEN PEAS

Along with providing vitamins, minerals, fibre and antioxidants, the humble green pea is a good source of protein. A serving of 175g of green peas (without the pod) will provide 8g of protein. Green peas can be used in soups, curries and omelettes or scrambles, as a side dish for dinner or in salads.

NUTS AND NUT BUTTERS

All nuts contain both healthy fats and protein, making them an important part of any healthy diet. They are particularly great for vegetarian diets, though, as not only are they highly nutritious, they also provide protein – 20g per 100g of nuts. Adding nuts to main meals and nut butters to your snacks is a great way of adding a little extra protein to your diet. Nut and nut butters are energy-dense, however, so don't fall into the trap of thinking a little is good so a lot must be better. Gorging on nuts can pile on the pounds!

4. FOOD TIMING

Your daily aim is to align your general eating practice to your level of physical activity, meaning you eat the type and amount of food that is specific to your individual needs. If you are sitting at a desk all day, your need for energy and carbohydrate is significantly less than a person who is on their feet all day and who completes high-intensity physical activity on four or more days per week. For pre-exercise meals, the guide is not to eat a large meal within two to three hours before your exercise. Post-exercise, eat within an hour of completing your session for the best recovery. If you are just doing light activity like a walk or gentle gym workout, an hour either side of the session is a reasonable amount of time to avoid a stomach upset.

REST DAY AND EXERCISE DAY RECIPES

The recipes in this book are split into two main categories based on the nutrition profile of the recipe.

Rest day recipes are nutritious lower-carbohydrate recipes suitable for less active days and recovery days.

Exercise day recipes are nutritious higher-carbohydrate recipes designed to energise the body and support recovery after exercise.

EXERCISE RECOVERY

RESTORE
depleted energy and
fuel (glycogen) stores.

REHYDRATE
to replace lost fluid.

REPAIR
damaged muscle tissue.

"HIGHER-CARBOHYDRATE RECIPES ARE APPROPRIATE FOR PEOPLE WHO HAVE EXERCISED THAT DAY OR **WHO HAVE EXPENDED A SIGNIFICANT AMOUNT OF ENERGY.**"

I have categorised each recipe based on the amount of carbohydrate it contains. Higher-carbohydrate recipes are appropriate for people who have exercised that day or who have expended a significant amount of energy through physical activity. For example, if you have completed a high-intensity interval session in the gym, gone for an intense 6–10km run or completed a 70-minute high-intensity team sport training session, then your

meals that day should contain a higher proportion of carbohydrate.

If you have not completed any physical activity other than walking, then your need for both energy and carbohydrate will be much lower. Of course, you can eat any recipe in the book on any given day if it fits your specific need for calories, but it's easier to make an informed recipe choice based on your goal.

> ❗ **REMEMBER**
> The framework is based on carbohydrate, not energy, so a meal that contains a low or moderate level of carbohydrate can still be high in energy! And, of course, portion size is also a critical factor when calculating your need for energy and macronutrients.

ACTIVITY	NAME	RECIPE TYPE	OBJECTIVE
Low and moderate levels of exercise	**Rest day recipes**	■ Lower carbohydrate ■ High protein ■ Higher fibre	■ Stable energy ■ Wellbeing ■ Health ■ Nourish
Moderate and high-intensity exercise	**Exercise day recipes**	■ Higher carbohydrate ■ High/moderate protein ■ Lower fibre	■ Energise ■ Fuel ■ Perform ■ Restore ■ Recover

Intense exercise lasting more than 60 minutes will lead to a significant glycogen deficit (your muscles use it as fuel during exercise). Glycogen is simply the state or form that carbohydrates take when they are in storage in the body, so it's important to refuel with carbohydrate after intense exercise, assuming you are training soon again in the following days. My recommendations for immediate post-exercise recovery will include a fast-digesting source of carbohydrate and a small amount of protein to initiate the recovery process and begin replenishing depleted glycogen stores. This period is when the body has the greatest ability to absorb nutrients and specifically carbohydrate (and protein – see below). The type of carbohydrate is particularly important during this phase.

Fast-digesting carbohydrate, such as white rice, will result in faster storage of glycogen compared to slow-digesting carbohydrate, such as sweet potato or brown rice. This is one of the only periods when a person/athlete should consume fast-digesting sources of carbohydrate like sweet snacks, which include raisins, flavoured milk, rice cakes or energy bars. In recent years, much has been made in the media and nutrition literature about taking advantage of the immediate post-exercise recovery window (30–60 minutes) – sometimes called the 'window of opportunity'. Taking fast-digesting carbohydrate foods after intense exercise is certainly important for athletes who don't have much time before the next training session or competition, but if you're not exercising again within 48 hours, a balanced meal of even slow-digesting carbohydrate like sweet potato and a quality protein source like wild salmon will suffice.

HYDRATION

Some dehydration is inevitable during intense exercise as it's hard to drink fluids at the rate that you lose them through sweating. Rehydration is therefore an immediate priority for anyone who has exercised. Depending on environmental conditions, body size and exercise intensity, you can lose anything from 1.5 litres to 4 litres during a workout. These fluids must be replaced at a ratio of 1–1.5 litres of fluid for every 1kg lost, meaning you need to drink more than 3 litres of fluid in some cases. A simple method for measuring your weight loss is to weigh yourself in minimal clothing pre-and post-exercise; this will help to guide your fluid replacement targets.

5. SUPPLEMENTS

Just like nutrition strategies, taking supplements for health and/or sports performance is evidence-based and pragmatic. There is no legal definition of what a supplement is but the International Olympic Committee consensus statement describes it like this: 'a food, food component, nutrient, or non-food compound that is purposefully ingested in addition to the habitually consumed diet with the aim of achieving a specific health and/or performance benefit'.

In most cases, people can meet their need for nutrients by following a varied and balanced diet, but if a person can't meet this need (for whatever reason) a supplement can offer a viable solution. Ideally, any supplement should only be consumed under the guidance of a qualified expert, such as a registered dietitian or a doctor. Here is a short list of supplements that you can consider for use under appropriate and individual circumstances:

1. Vitamin D
2. Protein supplements
3. Omega-3 fish oils

VITAMIN D

In recent years vitamin D, often called the sunshine vitamin, has been one of the most talked-about supplements in health-related media. Researchers are still trying to establish exactly how much vitamin D we require from our diet and whether we should be supplementing it during the winter months. There is no doubt that in certain parts of the world, due to climate, environmental, dietary and cultural factors, relative vitamin D deficiency is common and vitamin D should be taken in supplement form to meet the body's requirement. So, what about Ireland: do we need to supplement with vitamin D in the winter months and, if so, how much is enough or too much?

Although more and more foods are being fortified with vitamin D, e.g. milk and cereals, most of these foods still contain relatively small amounts. The foods that naturally contain the richest source of vitamin D include wild-caught oily fish, namely salmon, mackerel, bluefish, tuna and sardines, and cod liver oil. If you haven't been exposed to much sunshine over the course of the year, don't eat vitamin D-rich foods and don't take a multivitamin, then it's likely you need a vitamin D supplement during the later stages of the winter months.

The only way you can know for sure if you are deficient in vitamin D is to have your doctor test your blood levels. To be absolutely sure you're getting enough, I'd recommend taking a vitamin D supplement containing 1000 to 2000 IU daily during the winter months until the late spring or early summer. Look for the vitamin D3 (cholecalciferol) form as this is the most appropriate one to supplement with. Those with an extreme vitamin D deficiency require much greater doses, so if you think you may be deficient, it is best to see your doctor and get your levels checked.

PROTEIN SUPPLEMENTS

Should I use a protein supplement? This is one of the most common questions that I am asked by people looking to get in shape, or who have just started training. The reason this is high on everyone's radar is through clever marketing and exaggerated claims from many companies trying to sell protein-based products, and a trend towards viewing high protein intakes as a key to health and fitness. So why have powdered protein supplements become such a common sight in gyms and dressing rooms? More important, who needs added protein, and is a powdered supplement the best way to go?

Most people will have heard of whey protein, which in very basic terms is a protein fraction found in milk. The two main types of protein in milk are casein (80 per cent) and whey (20 per cent). It can be separated from the casein but is usually produced as a by-product of cheese making. Whey is the liquid left behind when milk curdles into cheese, and the protein powder is produced when the leftover liquid is dried and the non-protein material, i.e. fats, are removed.

Whey protein contains approximately 79g of protein per 100g of powder. In practical terms, one 'scoop' from a typical powdered supplement is about 30g of powder, giving 120 calories, 23g of protein. Whey protein is a complete protein, meaning that of it contains all the essential amino acids, and has a high biological value (a favourable overall amino acid profile). However as it contains dairy, it is not suitable for a vegan diet. For vegan protein sources see page 48.

Athletes across a range of sports will have common goals: to increase muscle mass, to improve strength and often to reduce fat mass. Both in terms of daily intake and eating around training sessions, the timing of intake, quantity, and quality of protein plays a key role in achieving these goals. As you know by now, there are numerous whole food options that can provide nutrient-rich sources of protein as quick snacks around sessions – milk, yoghurt, boiled eggs, cold meats, pulses and nuts. But a protein powder supplement can offer a practical, time-efficient and convenient method of meeting protein needs if you are time-poor or just don't have the high-protein foods to hand. This is particularly true for athletes who regularly train to a high intensity. Added to this, whey is richer than other protein powder sources because it contains

"ATHLETES ACROSS A RANGE OF SPORTS WILL HAVE COMMON GOALS: **TO INCREASE MUSCLE MASS, TO IMPROVE STRENGTH AND OFTEN TO REDUCE FAT MASS.**"

WHEY PROTEIN

PROS ✔	CONS ✘
Whey protein is convenient and easy to carry, cutting down on the need to prepare meals that contain a protein source.	Protein supplements can be expensive.
Whey protein is a flexible food which can be used to increase the protein content of meals like porridge, smoothies, pancakes and snack bars.	You can achieve your need for protein with a well-planned diet. Doing a bit of recreational training does not mean you that need a protein supplement.
Whey protein is light, transportable and can be put in a shaker or a small Tupperware and simply mixed with water or milk for an instant protein hit.	People can become reliant on protein powder to hit their protein needs, rather than investing time in food preparation and cooking.
If you find it difficult to meet your protein needs – for example in the case of loss of appetite or injury – whey protein is a complete protein that offers a simple solution to help hit total daily protein targets.	There is a risk of contamination with any supplement including whey protein. For this reason, it is important to be vigilant when choosing a protein supplement, particularly for athletes competing at an elite level who are regularly tested for prohibited substances.

branched-chain amino acids (BCAAs). One of these BCAAs, known as leucine, is the key amino acid for regulating growth and repair in response to exercise training.

Some women believe that they shouldn't take whey protein – probably for fear of turning into one of those muscle-bound beasts pictured on the tubs! (By the same token, some men seem to think that simply taking whey will make them bigger without doing the hard hours in the gym). There's no need for this concern, however, as women simply don't have the hormones to build those big, bulky muscles. Research has shown that women who take whey protein, follow a calorie-deficit diet and exercise regularly can lose body fat – whey reduces cravings and hunger pangs. Again, women don't 'need' to take a whey protein supplement, but it can certainly be a practical solution for busy women who want to consume a protein-based snack on the go.

The problem is that with busy lifestyles, and commitments to work, family and sport, convenience often wins over best practice. In these cases, a powdered whey protein supplement is a practical solution as a convenient snack or if you struggle to meet your individual protein needs. It's also easy to add to recipes – for high-protein snacks such as protein balls, protein bars, pancakes and smoothies, which you will find in this book. Another simple tip that's a favourite among athletes is to add a scoop of protein powder to your morning porridge, effortlessly increasing the protein content of your breakfast.

"THE PROBLEM IS THAT WITH BUSY LIFESTYLES, AND COMMITMENTS TO WORK, FAMILY AND SPORT, CONVENIENCE OFTEN WINS OVER BEST PRACTICE."

FISH OILS

Taking a fish oil supplement is one of the best ways to ensure you are getting enough omega-3 fats in your daily diet. Even when you're eating a diet rich in omega-3 fats it can still be difficult to balance up the ratio of omega-3 to omega-6 fatty acids. For this reason, a good-quality fish oil supplement can be an excellent way of helping you get the balance right. Look to get between 1.5 and 3.0g of omega-3 fatty acids per day if using a fish oil supplement.

PLANNING YOUR MEALS

If you create your own meal plan at the beginning of each week from my recipes you are far more likely to stick to eating healthy meals. Use these templates as inspiration to make your own meal plan that suits your schedule, needs and goals.

MEAL	AIM	FOOD TYPE
BREAKFAST	**A positive start to your day** that energises your body with slow-digesting foods that sustain you to lunch.	You need to include **protein** as part of your breakfast to keep you full and stabilise your energy levels. If you're exercising in the morning this will also maintain positive responses and adaptation from your training.
SNACKS	To **top up energy levels** and prevent overeating at main meals.	Snacks between main meals should generally be **low in calories** and contain a good source of protein. Beware of over-snacking, though – often snacks are low in protein, which can lead to overeating.
LUNCH	Lunch is one of the most important meals of the day to top up energy stores and help you meet your need for protein. It's also **vital to have a good lunch if you plan on doing an intense exercise session in the late afternoon** or early evening.	The food eaten at lunch should provide a good source of protein (>30g) as well as **slow-releasing energy from healthy fats** and slow-digesting carbohydrate foods. Vegetables complemented with some high-quality meat or fish is often a great option.

MEAL	AIM	FOOD TYPE
DINNER	Dinner is the third main meal of the day that should be based on a **combination of protein, carbohydrate, healthy fats and fibre-rich foods**.	The foods eaten will be based on foods like meat, fish or poultry. If you are vegan or vegetarian this will be a plant-based meal. **It should be consumed at least two hours before you go to bed**. It should also be tasty, nutrient-dense, filling and be enjoyed with family or friends.
PRE-BED	This meal is most specific to athletes or those who are aiming to gain muscle mass and have a high requirement of protein. This meal can contribute to athletes **hitting their critical protein needs**.	A meal **low in calories and high in slow-digesting protein** is ideal. This could be a serving of high protein or natural yoghurt with some berries.
PRE-WORKOUT	This should provide some carbohydrate to 'prime' the body for exercise and provide energy to the body during an exercise session.	A meal that contains **carbohydrate and protein and is low in fibre** and is easy to digest. This could be a granola/fruit and nut bar or a smoothie.
POST-WORKOUT	Recovery from moderate or intense exercise is enhanced in the one to two hours after intense exercise by eating a combination of **easy-to-digest carbohydrate and protein** foods.	A meal that is low in fibre and is easy to digest. It should also provide some protein. **This should be a recovery meal** like a recovery smoothie, fruit and yoghurt, milk, or a brown bread sandwich.

SAMPLE WEEKLY NEEDS

FITNESS | WEIGHT | STABILITY | HEALTH

DAY	EXERCISE TYPE		CARBOHYDRATE NEEDS	RECIPE TYPE
MONDAY	Resistance exercise		Moderate	▶
TUESDAY	Moderate aerobic exercise		Moderate	▶
WEDNESDAY	Rest day		Low	⏸
THURSDAY	High-intensity aerobic exercise (1-3 hours)		High	▶
FRIDAY	Resistance exercise		Moderate	▶
SATURDAY	Moderate aerobic exercise		Moderate	▶
SUNDAY	Rest day		Low	⏸

SAMPLE RECIPE PLAN

Meals	MONDAY	TUESDAY	WEDNESDAY	THURSDAY	FRIDAY
	Gym Day	Aerobic Session	Rest Day	Gym Day	Aerobic Session
Breakfast	Run down the stairs overnight oats (page 87)	Coconut porridge with toasted almonds (page 78)	Poached eggs with avocado and smoked salmon (page 90)	Breakfast 'go' bars (page 77)	Bircher muesli (page 74)
Snack	Nut-berry protein snack pot (page 234)	Blueberry banana bread with peanut butter (page 209)	Fruit and nut protein bars (page 231)	Mixed berry recovery smoothie (page 227)	Apple nut butter sandwich (page 205)
Lunch	Baked potato with red pepper hummus (page 107)	Autumn roast squash and quinoa salad (page 106)	Chicken apple walnut salad (page 112)	Prawn stir-fry (page 128)	Quinoa super salad (page 132)
Dinner	Sweet potato and carrot fish pie (page 181)	Burrito bowl (page 152)	Spicy cod with plum tomatoes (page 175)	Epic chicken tikka (page 165)	Spicy mince bonanza (page 176)

VEGETARIAN RECIPE PLAN

Meals	MONDAY	TUESDAY	WEDNESDAY	THURSDAY	FRIDAY
	Gym Day	Aerobic Session	Rest Day	Gym Day	Aerobic Session
Breakfast	Run down the stairs overnight oats (page 87)	Satisfying breakfast smoothie (page 92)	Breakfast 'go' bars (page 77)	Shredded nut granola with yoghurt (page 95)	Crunchy fruit and nut granola with yoghurt (page 80)
Snack	2 slices of blueberry banana bread with nut butter (page 209)	Fruit and nut protein bars with a glass of milk (page 231)	Avocado toast with cottage cheese (page 195)	Nut-berry protein snack pot (page 234)	2 crunchy chia quinoa bars with a glass of milk (page 223)
Lunch	Spicy baked eggs with beans (page 138)	No-fuss chickpea and carrot pilaf (page 187)	Super green frittata (page 99)	Baked potato with red pepper hummus (page 107)	Autumn roast squash and quinoa salad (page 106)
Dinner	Chickpea and lentil curry with quinoa (page 116)	Quinoa super salad (page 132)	Roast peppers with lentils and quinoa (page 171)	Autumn roast squash and quinoa salad (page 106)	Burrito bowl (page 152)

BEFORE YOU START

MEASUREMENTS

If you use a little less or a little more of certain ingredients it won't make a big difference to the outcome of the recipe. However, when it comes to incorporating things like spices or baking powder the following abbreviations are important.

Teaspoon = tsp
Tablespoon = tbsp
A pinch = ½ teaspoon

ESSENTIAL EQUIPMENT

Basic equipment is all you need to prepare and cook the majority of the recipes, but just to be sure, here is a list of essential kitchen equipment that I couldn't do without:

- A sharp knife
- A solid chopping board
- A large saucepan
- A small saucepan
- A large non-stick frying pan
- A smaller non-stick frying pan (for toasting nuts and seeds)
- A big, ovenproof baking dish
- A 20 x 20cm baking tray
- A clean jam jar with a lid (for dressings)

- A large mixing bowl
- A peeler
- A masher
- A spatula
- A whisk
- A wooden spoon
- A grater
- A blender (stick or food processor)
- Baking/greaseproof paper
- Clingfilm

BREAKFAST

Banana Oat Bake

SERVES	PREP TIME	COOKING TIME	CALORIES per serving (198g)	CARBS (g)	PROTEIN (g)	FAT (g)	FIBRE (g)
3	10 mins	25 mins	467	60	14	19	7.9

 Exercise Day Recipe

When your healthy and nutritious breakfast tastes like a dessert, you know you've got your combination of ingredients right! This banana oat bake is a fantastic sharing brunch meal for a family but can just as easily be used by an athlete who wants to fuel up for training, needs a quick pre-made breakfast or wants to carb load for a competition.

INGREDIENTS

1 tbsp coconut oil, melted
200g jumbo oats
250ml whole milk or
  almond milk
3 tbsp blueberries
  (optional)
2 tsp cinnamon
1 tbsp honey
1 tsp vanilla extract
a pinch of sea salt
1 tsp cinnamon
1 banana, peeled
3 tbsp flaked almonds
1 tbsp pumpkin seeds
1 tbsp flaked almonds

OPTIONAL TOPPINGS:

berries of all kinds
nut butter
natural yoghurt

PREPARATION

1. Preheat the oven to 180°C.
2. Lightly coat a baking dish with a little coconut oil.
3. Place the oats in a bowl and mix with the milk.
4. Scoop the mixed oats and milk into the baking dish and stir in the berries, if using.
5. Add the honey, vanilla, remaining coconut oil and salt and mix. Then sprinkle cinnamon on top.
6. Chop the banana and spread it out on top of the oat mix.
7. Place in the oven and bake for 20 minutes, then remove from the oven and sprinkle the pumpkin seeds and flaked almonds over the top. Place back in the oven and bake for 5 more minutes or until the top of the bake turns golden brown.
8. Serve warm with your choice of toppings.

 Tips

- Slow-releasing energy meal
- Excellent fuel-up recipe
- Adjust the toppings from berries to yoghurt to make into a higher-protein recipe
- Add more milk for a softer texture

Bircher Muesli

SERVES	PREP TIME	CALORIES per serving (210g)	CARBS (g)	PROTEIN (g)	FAT (g)	FIBRE (g)
4	5 mins	399	46	13	18	7.2

 Exercise Day Recipe

This is the original 'overnight oats' recipe – a delicious high-carbohydrate breakfast option that combines oats, fresh apple juice, nuts and seeds. Soaking oats and seeds overnight makes for a creamy texture and easy digestion. Bircher muesli keeps for five days in the fridge so you can grab it in the morning for a quick ready-to-go breakfast. It's also a good source of protein, which makes it ideal to eat pre- or post-exercise to maximise performance and recovery.

INGREDIENTS

200g jumbo porridge oats
200ml apple juice
200g plain natural whole
   milk yoghurt
100ml whole milk
30g desiccated coconut
20g chopped mixed nuts
20g ground almonds
15g poppy seeds
15g honey
juice of 1 lemon

PREPARATION

1. Mix all the ingredients in a large bowl, cover in clingfilm and leave in the fridge overnight.
2. The next morning, serve as it is or topped with chopped fresh fruit and a drizzle of honey.

Tips

- **Perfect pre- or post-exercise**
- **Easily digestible**

Quick and easy

Blueberry and Banana Oat Pancakes

SERVES	PREP TIME	COOKING TIME	CALORIES per serving (204g)	CARBS (g)	PROTEIN (g)	FAT (g)	FIBRE (g)
3	5 mins	10 mins	403	60	15	15	7.1

 Exercise Day Recipe

Who doesn't love pancakes? With a combination of seeds, berries, bananas and eggs, this recipe has the makings of a super-healthy breakfast. Pancakes are a great option for breakfast if you need something that is filling and will keep your energy levels stable. You can add whey to the mix if you want to increase the protein content or simply top them with Greek yoghurt. Get creative and colourful with your choice of toppings – from fresh fruit to natural yoghurt – to make this recipe your own.

INGREDIENTS
130g jumbo porridge oats
3 free range eggs
1 tbsp honey
2 bananas, peeled
3 tbsp milled seeds (optional)
50ml milk
½ teaspoon coconut oil, for frying
3 tbsp blueberries (plus more to serve)
honey and natural yoghurt, to serve

PREPARATION
1. Using a blender or food processor, blend the oats, eggs, honey, bananas, seeds and milk into a soft, thick consistency.
2. Tip the mixture into a bowl and mix in the blueberries with a large spoon.
3. Use a tablespoon or a ladle to dollop batter into a non-stick, very lightly oiled pan for each pancake. Cook until golden on both sides.
4. Serve with natural yoghurt, honey and more fresh berries.

Tips

- A healthy spin on the classic pancake stack breakfast
- High-carb content perfect to fuel your morning workout
- Good natural source of protein

Breakfast 'Go' Bars

MAKES	PREP TIME	COOKING TIME	CALORIES per serving (80g)	CARBS (g)	PROTEIN (g)	FAT (g)	FIBRE (g)
10 bars	10 mins	20 mins	377	27	10	25	7.2

 Rest Day Recipe

These breakfast bars are an ideal option for anyone who is in a rush in the morning and doesn't have time to sit and have their homemade muesli or porridge. They can also be used as an on-the-go snack or when recovering from exercise.

INGREDIENTS
150g oats
65g flaked almonds
2 tbsp flaxseeds
4 tbsp pumpkin seeds
¼ tsp cinnamon
¼ tsp sea salt
35g raisins
35g dried cranberries
4 tbsp honey
240g almond butter
50g coconut oil

PREPARATION
1. Preheat your oven to 200°C.
2. Mix all dry ingredients (including the dried fruits) in a large bowl.
3. Mix the honey, almond butter and coconut oil in a separate bowl until well blended.
4. Add this wet mixture to the dry ingredients, and mix well until all the ingredients are combined.
5. Spread the breakfast bar mixture onto a baking tray lined with greaseproof paper.
6. Bake in the oven for 20 minutes.
7. Remove from the oven and allow to cool fully before cutting into 10 bars. Store in an airtight tin for up to a week.

Excellent pre- or post-exercise snack

Tips

- Ideal option for an on-the-go, light and easy-to-grab breakfast
- Your energy boost comes from a combination of oats, honey and almond butter
- Provide both an energy hit and a healthy hit of fibre and vitamin E

Coconut Porridge with Toasted Almonds

SERVES	PREP TIME	COOKING TIME	CALORIES per serving (239g)	CARBS (g)	PROTEIN (g)	FAT (g)	FIBRE (g)
2	5 mins	10 mins	438	53	14	19	7

 Exercise Day Recipe

When it comes to a delicious porridge, it's often about the toppings you use to really bring a sense of enjoyment. Porridge is an excellent source of carbohydrate and also provides a decent hit of protein, which is often forgotten. The golden sultanas and cranberries bring out a lovely natural sweetness in this recipe which means you only need a little bit of honey. Use jumbo oats if you want a slower release of energy and a more filling effect. It takes longer for your body to break down these oats.

INGREDIENTS
100g oats
1 tbsp golden sultanas
1 tbsp dried cranberries
2 tbsp desiccated coconut
300ml whole milk (or water for fewer calories)
2 tbsp flaked almonds
1 tsp honey

OPTIONAL TOPPINGS:
blueberries
chopped banana

PREPARATION
1. Put the oats, sultanas, cranberries, coconut and milk into a medium-sized saucepan and cook on a medium heat for 7 to 8 minutes, stirring regularly.
2. While the porridge is cooking, place the flaked almonds in a small, dry non-stick frying pan and toast for 2 to 3 minutes till golden brown – don't take your eye off them as they can easily burn!
3. Once the porridge is cooked through, remove from the heat and pour into bowls to serve.
4. Sprinkle the almonds over the oats with a little honey, adding blueberries and banana if you wish.

Tips

- Provides carb and energy to sustain high-intensity exercise
- Use jumbo oats for longer and slower energy release
- Good source of antioxidants and vitamin E from the almonds

Crunchy Fruit and Nut Granola

SERVES	PREP TIME	COOKING TIME	CALORIES per serving (100g)	CARBS (g)	PROTEIN (g)	FAT (g)	FIBRE (g)
5	5 mins	25 mins	465	38	17	25	9

 Exercise Day Recipe

Granola is a great breakfast or snack option to have on exercise days. You can make it to suit your specific needs, i.e. more oats, dried fruit and honey if you want to fuel up on carbs, or more nuts, seeds and oils and less dried fruit and oats for a lower-carb option. Buckwheat is a gluten-free option which brings quality protein, fibre and antioxidants to the mix.

INGREDIENTS
100g jumbo oats
3 tbsp buckwheat
4 tbsp mixed nuts
3 tbsp flaked almonds
2 tbsp pumpkin seeds
1 tsp cinnamon
2 tbsp coconut oil
2 tbsp honey
2 tbsp olive oil
75g dried fruit mix

PREPARATION
1. Preheat the oven to 200°C.
2. Mix all dry ingredients, except for the dried fruit, in a large bowl.
3. Melt the coconut oil in a small pan over a medium heat, then stir in the honey and olive oil.
4. Pour this over the dry mix in the bowl, and stir well – it will be sticky! Transfer to a large baking dish lined with greaseproof paper and bake in the oven for 15 minutes. Don't be tempted to add the fruit until later as it will burn.
5. Take the dish out of the oven, stir through the dried fruit, then bake for another 10 minutes until the granola is a light brown colour.

Tips

- An energy-rich breakfast, great for fuelling an endurance-based workout
- Serve with natural yoghurt to increase the protein hit
- Increase your portion size for more carbs

Excellent source of carbohydrate

Flaxseed Porridge

SERVES	PREP TIME	COOKING TIME	CALORIES per serving (295g)	CARBS (g)	PROTEIN (g)	FAT (g)	FIBRE (g)
2	4 mins	5 mins	295	9.4	22	19	8.7

 Rest Day Recipe

Flaxseed porridge is a great low-carb, high-fat and protein-rich alternative to traditional porridge oats. Flaxseeds and chia seeds provide plenty of healthy fats and 100 per cent of your daily recommended amount of omega-3. Chia seeds pack a strong punch for their size and are a vegan-friendly option for increasing both fibre and protein in the diet. The cacao nibs will also give you an antioxidant boost.

INGREDIENTS
2 tbsp flaxseeds
2 tbsp chia seeds (ground or whole)
250ml milk/almond milk (or 100 ml coconut milk mixed with 150ml water)
1 scoop whey protein powder (vanilla or chocolate)
1 tbsp cinnamon
1 tbsp cacao nibs
1 tbsp desiccated coconut

PREPARATION
1. In a medium-sized pot on a low heat, combine all the ingredients except for the cacao nibs and coconut.
2. Stir frequently for 5 minutes or until thick and bubbling.
3. Remove from the heat and serve with cacao nibs and desiccated coconut sprinkled on top.

Tips

- Ideal for rest days as it contains high-quality fats from flaxseeds and chia seeds
- Customise by adding your favourite protein powder flavour
- Low-carbohydrate, heart-healthy breakfast option

Eggy Bacon Muffins

SERVES	PREP TIME	COOKING TIME	CALORIES per serving (100g)	CARBS (g)	PROTEIN (g)	FAT (g)	FIBRE (g)
6	10 mins	12 mins	100	1.7	8.7	6.5	1.2

 Rest Day Recipe

These nutritious eggy veggie buns tick all the right boxes for a healthy snack, whether eaten hot out of the oven, or later on the go. If you are feeling peckish before bed, these would also work well as a pre-bedtime snack. They are low in carbohydrate, rich in protein and essential fats and vitamins, while the addition of vegetables rounds them off nicely. Switch this recipe up by using whatever vegetables you have to hand.

INGREDIENTS

1 red pepper, deseeded and
  chopped
2 spring onions, sliced
2 handfuls of baby spinach,
  washed and chopped
2 slices of cooked bacon
  or good-quality ham,
  chopped into small pieces
4 free range eggs
sea salt and freshly ground
  black pepper
a pinch of cayenne pepper
  (optional)

PREPARATION

1. Preheat the oven to 180°C. Line a muffin tin with 12 muffin cases (silicon cases work great here).
2. In a small bowl, mix the pepper, spring onions, spinach and bacon or ham together.
3. Spoon a small amount of this mixture evenly into the bottom of each muffin case.
4. Beat the eggs and season with salt, pepper and optional cayenne pepper.
5. Pour this evenly over the mixture in the muffin cases so that each one is nearly full.
6. Bake in the oven for 12 minutes and serve, or store in an airtight container for later.

Tips

- A low-calorie breakfast with a protein kick to set you on your way
- Ideal late-night recovery snack
- Leave out the bacon for a vegetarian option

Homemade Muesli

SERVES	PREP TIME	CALORIES per serving (99g)	CARBS (g)	PROTEIN (g)	FAT (g)	FIBRE (g)
5	10 mins	420	43	17	20	9.2

 Exercise Day Recipe

I am biased, but in my opinion there is nothing like your own homemade muesli for taste or nutrition value. You can make it in large batches for a quick breakfast, and it's better value than shop-bought muesli. This recipe combines healthy fats from the nuts, an excellent source of plant protein from the shelled hemp seeds and slow-releasing energy from the oats.

INGREDIENTS
4 tbsp milled flaxseeds
50g sliced or flaked almonds
50g pumpkin seeds
30g shelled hemp seeds
20g raw peanuts
200g jumbo rolled oats
50g dried cranberries
20g raisins
20g desiccated coconut or coconut flakes

PREPARATION
1. Place all the nuts and seeds in a dry, non-stick frying pan and toast over a medium heat for 5 minutes until taking on some colour.
2. Transfer to a mixing bowl and stir through the oats, dried fruit and coconut. Pour into an airtight container and enjoy with milk or yoghurt and fresh fruit for breakfast.

Excellent source of natural protein and fibre

Tips

- Great source of slow-digesting carbohydrate
- Action-packed with healthy fats from a variety of nuts and seeds
- High in omega-3 and omega-6 essential fatty acids
- Increase the portion size for more carbs

Pitta Pocket Breakfast

SERVES	PREP TIME	COOKING TIME	CALORIES per serving (184g)	CARBS (g)	PROTEIN (g)	FAT (g)	FIBRE (g)
2	3 – 4 mins	10 mins	575	37	28	33	8.7

 Exercise Day Recipe

The pitta pocket breakfast offers a creative way to shake up scrambled egg. Chorizo, egg and avocado combine really well to deliver great flavour and high-quality proteins and fats. Eggs are known as a complete source of protein as they provide all nine essential amino acids and avocados are a good source of monosaturated healthy fat.

INGREDIENTS

50g chorizo, chopped
4 free range eggs, beaten
2 wholemeal pittas
1 avocado, split, stone
 removed and flesh
 scooped out
2 handfuls of rocket
freshly ground black
 pepper

PREPARATION

1. Put the chorizo in a dry, non-stick pan on a medium heat and fry until crisp; be careful not to burn it. Set chorizo aside and discard the excess oil.
2. Add the beaten egg to the pan and stir gently with a wooden spoon until scrambled. Stir the chorizo through the egg just before it's finished cooking.
3. Toast the pittas, then mash the avocado with a fork and spread along the inside of each one. Add a handful of rocket to each pocket and then fill with the chorizo scramble.
4. Season with cracked black pepper and serve.

 Tips

- Provides high-quality healthy fats and a moderate amount of carbohydrate

Great post-exercise recovery meal

Poached Eggs with Avocado and Smoked Salmon

SERVES	PREP TIME	COOKING TIME	CALORIES per serving (173g)	CARBS (g)	PROTEIN (g)	FAT (g)	FIBRE (g)
2	10 mins	10 mins	283	9.1	22	18	2.3

 Rest Day Recipe

Tucking into some nicely cooked poached eggs with avocado and smoked salmon is a great way to start your day. It works particularly well when you have time at the weekend to sit and enjoy it. This is a high-protein and omega-3-rich breakfast which will help to stabilise your energy levels and fill you up for hours.

INGREDIENTS
100g smoked salmon
2 large free range eggs
a ripe avocado, sliced
toasted or freshly made
 brown bread
juice of ½ a lemon
sea salt and freshly ground
 black pepper

PREPARATION
1. Prepare 2 smoked salmon slices.
2. Poach the 2 eggs in simmering water for 3 to 4 minutes (silicone pouches work great here if you're not an adept egg-poacher!)
3. Divide the sliced avocado and smoked salmon between two slices of toast or homemade bread and add a squeeze of lemon juice to each.
4. Place your poached eggs on top of the smoked salmon and serve with a little salt and pepper.

Tips

- Poached eggs, avocado and salmon is a filling breakfast with an array of healthy minerals, fats and a quality source of protein
- Good source of vitamin D and omega-3 healthy fats

Low-carbohydrate breakfast option

Satisfying Breakfast Smoothie

SERVES	PREP TIME	CALORIES per serving (377g)	CARBS (g)	PROTEIN (g)	FAT (g)	FIBRE (g)
1	2 mins	501	49	26	21	4.9

 Exercise Day Recipe

This breakfast smoothie does exactly what it promises: it will leave you satisfied and full. Grab it on your way out for a quick breakfast on the go, or have it before you leave the house. To ensure that your smoothie has a balance of healthy fats and protein I've added avocado, Greek yoghurt and whey powder to the mix.

INGREDIENTS
150 ml whole milk
2 tbsp oats
1 tsp coconut oil
1 scoop of vanilla whey
   protein powder
1 banana
½ a ripe avocado
1 tbsp Greek yoghurt
1 tsp honey
a sprinkle of ground
   cinnamon
1–2 ice cubes

PREPARATION
1. Whizz all ingredients together in a blender and serve.
2. For a thicker or thinner smoothie, adjust the amount of milk and ice cubes to suit your preference.

 Tips

- Ideal for a quick on-the-go breakfast
- Avocado and Greek yoghurt provide healthy fats
- If you prefer a lower-calorie, lighter smoothie, reduce the avocado to 1 tbsp

Great
pre-gym
meal

Spanish Tortilla Loaf

SERVES	PREP TIME	COOKING TIME	CALORIES per serving (283g)	CARBS (g)	PROTEIN (g)	FAT (g)	FIBRE (g)
4	10 mins	40 mins	455	20	18	34	2.5

 Rest Day Recipe

Want a breakfast that will keep you going till lunch and beyond? This Spanish tortilla loaf won't disappoint you, I promise. It's high in energy, protein and healthy fats that will keep you feeling full for hours. This is a meal that works perfectly at the weekend to savour and enjoy yourself or with family members. It can of course be enjoyed as a vegetarian meal too as there is no meat.

INGREDIENTS

3 medium potatoes, cut into thin slices
30g butter
3 tbsp olive oil
1 medium-sized onion, peeled and chopped
2 cloves of garlic, peeled and chopped
6 large free range eggs
2 tbsp sour cream
sea salt and freshly ground black pepper
50g mature Cheddar cheese, grated

PREPARATION

1. Steam the potatoes over a pot of gently simmering water for about 20 minutes, until softened.
2. Preheat the oven to 190°C. Grease a narrow 23 x 13cm loaf tin with the butter.
3. Heat the olive oil in a frying pan over a medium heat. Add the onion and garlic and cook for 2 to 3 minutes. Put the potatoes, onions and garlic in the greased tin, spreading them out evenly.
4. Beat the eggs in a large bowl, then mix in the sour cream and season with salt and pepper. Pour this over the potatoes and mix gently.
5. Cook your loaf in the oven for 25 minutes. Remove from the oven, scatter the grated Cheddar on top, then cook for another 15 minutes, until the egg is completely cooked through.
6. Rest for 10 minutes, then carefully invert the loaf over a board or large plate (it should come out easily if you've greased the tin enough). Cut into thick slices and serve.

Tips

- **Provides high-quality healthy fats and a moderate amount of carbohydrate**

Shredded Nut Granola

SERVES	PREP TIME	COOKING TIME	CALORIES per serving (69g)	CARBS (g)	PROTEIN (g)	FAT (g)	FIBRE (g)
2	10 mins	20 mins	649	30	22	49	8.4

 Rest Day Recipe

This nutty granola is perfect for anyone looking for a low-carbohydrate, high-energy breakfast. The cinnamon and vanilla extract combine with the toasted nuts and seeds to give a wonderful flavour. The mixture of nuts provides an excellent source of the mineral copper, which plays a role in supporting your immune system.

INGREDIENTS
75g mixed nuts, chopped
40g jumbo porridge oats
2 tbsp buckwheat
1 tbsp pumpkin seeds
1 tbsp sunflower seeds
2 tsp desiccated coconut
2 tsp shelled hemp seeds
1 tsp cinnamon
2 tsp coconut oil
2 tsp vanilla extract

PREPARATION
1. Preheat the oven to 160°C.
2. Mix all the dry ingredients in a bowl.
3. Melt the coconut oil over a low heat, mix in the vanilla extract and stir into the dry mix.
4. Spread the mix flat on a baking tray lined with greaseproof paper and bake for 20 minutes in the oven, until crunchy and golden. Allow to cool before serving. Store in an airtight container.

Tips

- Low-carb and a great natural source of plant protein
- Ideal for recovery or rest days
- Works great as a yoghurt topper

High-energy breakfast

Smoky Bacon Sweet Potato Cakes

SERVES	PREP TIME	COOKING TIME	CALORIES per serving (357g)	CARBS (g)	PROTEIN (g)	FAT (g)	FIBRE (g)
2	10 mins	30 mins	460	51	14	22	6.3

 Exercise Day Recipe

These smoky sweet potato cakes are delicious for breakfast or brunch. You may need a bit more time to prep and cook them but they are certainly worth the wait. They offer a good source of protein from the egg and bacon, and a reasonable amount of carbohydrate from the sweet potato tops up energy levels and keeps you feeling full.

INGREDIENTS

2 medium sweet potatoes, peeled and thinly sliced
½ tbsp olive oil
4 slices of smoked bacon, chopped
1 onion, peeled and diced
4 fresh basil leaves
1 free range egg, beaten
½ tsp smoked paprika
a pinch of sea salt and freshly ground black pepper
1 tbsp coconut oil

PREPARATION

1. Steam the sweet potato slices over a pot of gently simmering water for approximately 20 minutes until soft.
2. In the meantime, heat the oil in a pan and fry the bacon, onion and basil over a medium to high heat until the onions are brown and the bacon crisp.
3. Mash the cooked sweet potatoes in a large bowl with the egg.
4. Add the cooked bacon mix to the bowl and season with smoked paprika, salt and pepper, then use a tablespoon to form the mixture into 4 'cakes'.
5. In a large pan over a medium to high heat, melt a knob of coconut oil and fry the cakes until the outsides are golden and the insides are heated through – about 4 minutes each side.
6. Enjoy as they are or serve with scrambled egg and sliced avocado.

Tips

- A slow energy-releasing meal
- Sweet potatoes are an excellent source of vitamin A
- Omit the bacon to make the cakes vegetarian

Good source of fibre and protein

Sweet Potato Hash with Baked Eggs

SERVES	PREP TIME	COOKING TIME	CALORIES per serving (393g)	CARBS (g)	PROTEIN (g)	FAT (g)	FIBRE (g)
3	5 mins	20 mins	428	39	20	22	7.2

 Exercise Day Recipe

The combination of sweet potatoes, baked eggs and Cheddar cheese in this recipe tastes delicious. This could easily become one of your favourite breakfast options as it is easy to eat first thing in the morning and keeps you satisfied for hours. The eggs will deliver a complete source of protein, while the spinach and vegetables hit you with an array of essential minerals and vitamins.

INGREDIENTS

1 tbsp coconut oil or olive oil
1 medium onion, peeled and finely sliced
4 cloves of garlic, peeled and chopped
¼ tsp sea salt
¼ tsp freshly ground black pepper
2 medium sweet potatoes, peeled and cut into small cubes
¼ tsp cayenne pepper
¼ tsp smoked paprika
1 medium red pepper, deseeded and sliced
100g spinach, washed and coarsely shredded
3 free range eggs
100g strong Cheddar cheese, grated

PREPARATION

1. Preheat the oven to 180°C.
2. Heat the oil over a medium to low heat in a large non-stick pan. Add the onion, garlic, salt and pepper and sauté for a minute until beginning to soften.
3. Add the sweet potato and cook until it has softened, stirring often. This should take around 10 minutes.
4. Sprinkle everything in the pan with the cayenne pepper and smoked paprika. Add the red pepper and cook for about 2 minutes until tender. Add the spinach and cook until wilted.
5. Crack the 3 eggs over the hash, scatter the cheese on top then place the skillet/pan in the oven for roughly 5 to 6 minutes until the eggs are set and the cheese is bubbling.

Note: Only bake in the oven if your skillet/pan has a metal handle. Otherwise place under a preheated grill.

Tips

- Versatile meal which could be used for breakfast or before a workout – just leave time for it to digest
- Light on the stomach and provides slow-releasing carbs to fuel an active day ahead
- High in a range of minerals and vitamins including vitamins A, C, D and K

LUNCH

Almond-Covered Fried Chicken

SERVES	PREP TIME	COOKING TIME	CALORIES per serving (220g)	CARBS (g)	PROTEIN (g)	FAT (g)	FIBRE (g)
2	10 mins	20 mins	461	3.9	44	30	5.8

 Rest Day Recipe

This recipe is a healthy and tasty alternative to breaded fried chicken, using ground almond flour and coconut oil. It is high in protein and the almond flour provides a good source of healthy fats. This combination also has a strong effect on satisfying your appetite. Importantly, this recipe can be reheated when time is short, so you'll never opt for processed fast food again!

INGREDIENTS
2 free range chicken fillets
1 free range egg
2 tbsp whole milk or
  almond milk
80g almond flour or ground
  almonds
1 tsp paprika
sea salt
freshly ground black
  pepper
coconut oil for frying

PREPARATION
1. Preheat your oven to 190°C.
2. Slice each chicken fillet lengthways into 2 even strips.
3. In a shallow bowl, whisk the egg and milk together.
4. Combine the flour/ground almonds and seasoning in another shallow bowl.
5. Dip a chicken strip into the egg mixture, transfer to the flour mix and coat generously. Set aside on a plate and repeat for the remaining strips.
6. Melt some coconut oil in a large, non-stick pan over a high heat and fry the chicken for 2 to 3 minutes each side until turning golden and crisp.
7. Transfer to a baking sheet and place in the oven for 10 minutes until the chicken is cooked through and golden brown on the outside. Serve with roast vegetables and baked sweet or regular potato.

Tips

- Low-carbohydrate option
- Perfect Friday or Saturday evening dish for that 'takeaway' feel

A high-protein super-tasty meal

Autumn Roast Squash and Quinoa Salad

SERVES	PREP TIME	COOKING TIME	CALORIES per serving (620g)	CARBS (g)	PROTEIN (g)	FAT (g)	FIBRE (g)
4	10 mins	25 mins	427	49	15	20	14

 Exercise Day Recipe

Roasted squash mixed through a salad is a game changer in terms of flavour and adding colour. This meat-free, vegetarian-friendly salad contains carbohydrates, mostly from the quinoa, and fats from the feta cheese. Due to the high amount of carbs and fibre this salad would work well as a recovery meal following exercise.

INGREDIENTS

1 large butternut squash, chopped
3 medium carrots, chopped
1 tbsp olive oil (plus more for sautéing)
2 tbsp balsamic vinegar
¼ tsp chilli flakes
¼ tsp ground cumin
¼ tsp smoked paprika
a pinch of sea salt
1 red onion, peeled and chopped

3 cloves of garlic, peeled and finely chopped
a head of broccoli, florets roughly chopped
½ a courgette, chopped
250ml water
200g quinoa
a bunch of spinach leaves, washed
8 cherry tomatoes, chopped
50g feta cheese, chopped into cubes

3 tbsp chopped almonds, toasted in a dry frying pan

FOR THE DRESSING:

3 tbsp olive oil
3 tbsp balsamic vinegar
1 tbsp honey
1 tsp mustard
a squeeze of lime juice
a squeeze of lemon juice

PREPARATION

1. Preheat the oven to 190°C.
2. In a large bowl, toss the butternut squash and carrots with the olive oil, balsamic vinegar, chilli flakes, cumin, smoked paprika and salt. Transfer to a baking tray lined with greaseproof paper and put in the oven for 25 minutes.
3. Meanwhile heat some oil in a large non-stick pan over a medium heat, add the onion and garlic and sauté for 3 to 4 minutes.
4. Add the broccoli and courgette to the pan and cook for 2 to 3 minutes.
5. Pour the water into the pan then add the quinoa. Simmer for another 7 to 8 minutes.
6. Now you're ready to assemble your salad. Get a large bowl and put in the spinach leaves, chopped tomatoes, roasted squash and carrots and the broccoli, courgette and quinoa mixture.
7. Scatter the feta cheese cubes and toasted almonds over the top.
8. Put all the dressing ingredients into a clean jar, put the lid on and shake well. Taste and adjust for degree of sweetness desired.

Baked Potato with Red Pepper Hummus

SERVES	PREP TIME	COOKING TIME	CALORIES per serving (523g)	CARBS (g)	PROTEIN (g)	FAT (g)	FIBRE (g)
2	5 mins	60 mins	553	62	17	23	13

 Exercise Day Recipe

Baked potato combines brilliantly with hummus to give you a tasty and nourishing meal. This is an excellent fuel-up or post-workout recovery meal that takes very little preparation. All you need to do is scale up the portion size if you need more carbohydrate and protein to meet your nutrient targets.

INGREDIENTS

2 large baking potatoes, scrubbed

For the hummus:
300g tinned chickpeas
1 tbsp tahini
2 tbsp olive oil
1 garlic clove, peeled and chopped
½ red pepper, deseeded and roughly chopped
⅓ tsp cumin
⅓ tsp paprika
⅓ tsp sea salt
juice of ½ a lime
sea salt and freshly ground black pepper, to serve

PREPARATION

1. Preheat your oven to 190°C.
2. Place the potatoes in the oven and bake for 60 minutes or until they are tender and a skewer goes in easily.
3. Meanwhile make the hummus. Put all the ingredients in a food processor or blender and blend till smooth. Tip: If you have the time, roast the pepper with a little olive oil and salt for 5 to 6 minutes before adding to the blender with the rest of the hummus ingredients. It brings a little more depth of flavour and sweetness to the dish.
4. Place the baked potatoes on a plate, split them open, and scoop the hummus over the top.
5. Add salt and pepper to serve if you like.

Tips

- Great option for recovery following a workout
- Meat-free meal with a good source of protein
- Meal with fast-releasing carbs

Beef Bolognese

SERVES	PREP TIME	COOKING TIME	CALORIES per serving (740g)	CARBS (g)	PROTEIN (g)	FAT (g)	FIBRE (g)
2	5 mins	20 mins	641	49	65	22	9

 Exercise Day Recipe

Everyone needs a killer Bolognese recipe in their repertoire that is fast to whip up but still tastes great. Beef Bolognese packs a strong protein hit with 44g of protein, with the majority of this coming from high-quality minced beef. Bolognese goes down a treat and is easily digestible. This meal works well in the four hours before or the two hours after exercise.

INGREDIENTS

1 tbsp olive oil
2 cloves of garlic, peeled and crushed
1 onion, peeled and diced
500g good-quality lean beef mince
1 tbsp Worcestershire sauce
sea salt and freshly ground black pepper
1 red pepper, deseeded and diced
1 carrot, grated
1 400g tin of chopped tomatoes
1 tsp dried oregano
1 tsp dried basil
160g pasta of choice (spaghetti is the traditional choice)
40g Parmesan cheese, grated (optional)

PREPARATION

1. Heat the olive oil in a large pan on a medium to high heat. Add the garlic and onion and sauté until softened, about 5 minutes.
2. Next add the mince and Worcestershire sauce, breaking up the meat with a wooden spoon as it browns. Season well with the salt and pepper.
3. Once the beef has browned, add in the diced pepper, grated carrot, tinned tomatoes and herbs. Stir everything together well.
4. Bring to the boil then reduce the heat and simmer gently for 20 minutes.
5. While the sauce is cooking, bring a large pot of salted water to the boil. Add your pasta of choice to the pot and cook for the amount of time it says on the packet. Drain well, then add to the meat sauce.
6. Take the pan off the heat and stir everything together well. Divide the Bolognese between 3 bowls and sprinkle cheese on top, if using. Finish with a few grinds of black pepper.

Tips

- The beef offers a good source of protein and the pasta provides plenty of carbohydrate – increase the pasta portion for more carbs
- Low in fibre and when combined with pasta or rice the sauce is a good option to consume before training
- Provides all your daily recommended amount for vitamin C

Chicken and Broccoli Salad with Peanut Dressing

SERVES	PREP TIME	CALORIES per serving (279g)	CARBS (g)	PROTEIN (g)	FAT (g)	FIBRE (g)
3	10 mins	465	19	32	30	9.1

 Rest Day Recipe

Who knew peanut butter in a salad could be so good? But once you've tasted it, you'll know that this recipe just makes complete sense! Not to mention that it packs its weight in protein too. This is a proper salad, delicious, satisfying and rich in vitamins, minerals and antioxidants.

INGREDIENTS

1 large head broccoli, cut into small florets
1 cooked free range chicken breast fillet, chopped
1 cup shelled, cooked edamame beans (available frozen in Asian supermarkets)
½ a red onion, thinly sliced
20g cashew nuts
20g hazelnuts

For the dressing:

3 tbsp peanut butter
1 tbsp rice vinegar
1 tbsp soy sauce
1 tbsp honey
1/8 teaspoon toasted sesame oil
1–2 tbsp hot water, as needed, to thin the dressing
sesame seeds, to garnish

PREPARATION

1. Boil a kettle of water. Put the broccoli in a colander and slowly pour the boiling water over to blanch it, then allow to cool. (If you need to cool the broccoli quickly, place it in the fridge until it's cold.)
2. Once cooled, put into a big salad bowl and toss with the remaining salad ingredients until well combined.
3. Now make the peanut dressing. Whisk all the dressing ingredients together until combined. If the dressing is too thick, whisk in hot water a tablespoon at a time until it reaches the desired consistency.
4. Pour the peanut dressing over the salad and mix well. Serve immediately, garnished with the sesame seeds.

 Tips

- **Be mindful of portion control – it's particularly delicious!**
- **Excellent source of healthy fats**

Chicken and Goat's Cheese Salad with Toasted Nuts

SERVES	PREP TIME	COOKING TIME	CALORIES per serving (322g)	CARBS (g)	PROTEIN (g)	FAT (g)	FIBRE (g)
3	10 mins	20 mins	545	22	24	41	6.5

 Rest Day Recipe

This protein-boosting chicken apple salad with delicious apple-mint vinaigrette is truly satisfying. The mix of fresh leaves, nuts and apple provide a huge nutrient punch and the chicken supplies one of your daily protein hits! Added to that, both pecan and macadamia nuts provide energy and healthy fats to keep you satisfied.

INGREDIENTS
1 large free range chicken breast
1 clove of garlic, peeled and
  chopped
sea salt
a pinch of paprika
a small bunch of spinach
  leaves, washed
a small bunch of rocket leaves,
  washed
a small bunch of baby kale,
  washed and chopped

1 large apple, cored and sliced
1 small red onion, peeled and
  finely diced
40g pickled cucumber, sliced
50g goat's cheese
2 tbsp pecan nuts
2 tbsp macadamia nuts or
  hazelnuts
1 tbsp flaked almonds
1 tsp honey

For the dressing:
juice of 1 lime
1 tbsp fresh mint leaves,
  chopped
20ml apple juice
2 tbsp olive oil
2 tbsp apple cider vinegar
1 tsp honey

PREPARATION
1. Preheat the oven to 200°C. Put the chicken breast in a small baking dish, drizzle with olive oil and scatter over the salt and paprika. Bake for approximately 20 minutes. (If you wish, you could prepare this ahead of time and have it ready in the fridge.)
2. Meanwhile, mix all the salad dressing ingredients together in a small bowl to allow the ingredients to combine. Set aside.
3. In a large bowl, mix the spinach, rocket and kale, apple, onion and pickled cucumber. Crumble in the goat's cheese.
4. In a dry frying pan, toast the pecans and macadamia nuts or hazelnuts over a gentle heat with a little honey for 7 to 8 minutes until fragrant and starting to turn light brown. Don't let them burn! When cooled, add to the salad bowl.
5. Toast the flaked almonds separately for 5 minutes.
6. Remove the chicken from the oven, cut it into strips, add it to the salad and mix well.
7. Pour the dressing over the salad, scatter over the toasted almonds, mix gently and serve.

Chicken Apple Walnut Salad

SERVES	PREP TIME	CALORIES per serving (672g)	CARBS (g)	PROTEIN (g)	FAT (g)	FIBRE (g)
1	10 mins	721	34	55	42	9.6

 Rest Day Recipe

The chicken apple walnut salad is easily put together and is a good packed lunch option that uses up any leftover chicken from the night before. This meal would be a good option to have on a recovery day and the nuts provide a great source of healthy fats.

INGREDIENTS

1 free range chicken breast
  fillet, cooked and sliced
a handful of baby spinach
  leaves, washed
a handful of rocket leaves,
  washed
1 medium apple, cored and
  sliced
70g roasted pickled
  beetroot, sliced
100g pickled cucumber
15g walnuts
10g raw peanuts
40g feta cheese

For the dressing:
1 tbsp olive oil
10ml apple juice
a handful of fresh parsley,
  chopped
a handful of fresh mint
  leaves, chopped

PREPARATION

1. Place the chicken, spinach, rocket, apple, beetroot, cucumber and nuts in a medium salad bowl and mix gently.
2. Put the dressing ingredients in a small bowl and mix well.
3. Crumble the feta into the salad, then pour the dressing over. Toss everything together before serving.

Tips

• Offers a moderate amount of carbs but a big protein hit
• High in vitamin K, which is good for immune and bone health

Chicken, Peanut and Baby Bok Choy Salad

SERVES	PREP TIME	COOKING TIME	CALORIES per serving (436g)	CARBS (g)	PROTEIN (g)	FAT (g)	FIBRE (g)
2	10 mins	20 mins	448	11	36	29	8.4

 Rest Day Recipe

This salad would be ideal to bring to work if you're having a rest day and do not require a heavy carbohydrate-based meal. Peanuts combine surprisingly well with the other ingredients and offer a rich source of healthy fats. This salad is high in protein and would work well for those trying to control their calorie intake but still satisfy their taste buds.

INGREDIENTS
15g raw peanuts

15g hazelnuts

30g mangetout

a large free range chicken breast fillet, grilled or baked and chopped

4 baby bok choy, cleaned of all grit, cut in half lengthwise and shredded

½ a green pepper, deseeded and chopped

½ a red pepper, deseeded and chopped

70g radishes, finely sliced

3 spring onions, finely sliced

For the dressing:
20ml sesame oil

a squeeze of lime juice

½ a red chilli, deseeded and chopped

a small bunch of fresh coriander

a pinch of sea salt

PREPARATION
1. Toast the peanuts and hazelnuts in a dry frying pan for about 8 minutes, shaking once or twice. Set aside and when cool, chop them roughly.
2. Bring a small pot of salted water to the boil and blanch the mangetout for 2 minutes – they should still retain a 'bite'. Rinse them immediately in cold water, drain and place in a large mixing bowl along with the chicken, bok choy and chopped peppers.
3. Add the sliced radishes and spring onion to the bowl.
4. Take half of the chopped roasted peanuts and hazelnuts and add to the bowl too, mixing everything together gently.
5. To make the dressing, blend the sesame oil, lime juice, chilli, fresh coriander and salt in a food processor (or using a stick blender).
6. Next blend the remaining half of the nuts into the dressing until smooth, forming a paste. Spoon the dressing over the salad and fold it in gently to distribute evenly.

Tips

- **Low-carbohydrate meal**
- **Packs a big protein hit**
- **Excellent source of vitamin C**

Chickpea and Lentil Curry with Quinoa

SERVES	PREP TIME	COOKING TIME	CALORIES per serving (930g)	CARBS (g)	PROTEIN (g)	FAT (g)	FIBRE (g)
2	10 mins	35 mins	588	80	34	16	25

 Exercise Day Recipe

Chickpea lentil curry, one of my main go-to meat-free meals, is a dish everyone can appreciate and enjoy. Chickpeas go really well with curry and offer a rich source of protein. They are also the main source of carbohydrate in this recipe, alongside quinoa. As the curry is high in fibre it can also be used as a recovery option rather than a pre-exercise meal.

INGREDIENTS

1 onion, peeled and chopped
3 cloves of garlic, peeled and chopped
2 red chillis, deseeded and finely chopped
1 tbsp olive oil
a pinch of sea salt
1 red pepper, deseeded and chopped
1 green pepper, deseeded and chopped
½ a courgette, chopped
1 400g tin of tomatoes
½ tsp ground cumin
½ tsp paprika
½ tsp ground turmeric
1 tsp garam masala
1 tbsp curry powder
a handful of fresh coriander, chopped
150g lentils
150g quinoa
1 400g tin of chickpeas, drained
Greek yoghurt, to serve

PREPARATION

1. In a large saucepan on a medium heat, fry the chopped onion, garlic and chilli in the olive oil with a pinch of salt until softened.
2. Add the chopped peppers and courgette and stir. Cook for 3 to 4 minutes until they also begin to turn soft.
3. Add the tinned tomatoes, mix, then stir in all the spices and the chopped coriander.
4. Pour in the lentils and stir well.
5. In another medium-sized saucepan, boil 300ml of water, then add the quinoa and cook until nearly all the water has been absorbed and the quinoa is fluffy, about 15 minutes. *Tip: Cook the quinoa in vegetable stock if you prefer; this will add a bit more flavour.*
6. Add the chickpeas to the curry mix and stir well. Simmer for about 20 minutes until the lentils are soft.
7. Serve the curry on a bed of quinoa topped with a little Greek yoghurt.

Tips

- **High-carbohydrate meal ideal for exercise recovery**
- **Good plant-based protein meal**

Competition Day Chicken Noodles

SERVES	PREP TIME	COOKING TIME	CALORIES per serving (375g)	CARBS (g)	PROTEIN (g)	FAT (g)	FIBRE (g)
2	10 mins	10 mins	648	60	58	19	3

 Exercise Day Recipe

This dish is a firm favourite with many elite athletes because it's easy to make, tastes fantastic, feels light in the tummy and ticks all the boxes for a pre-competition or high-intensity exercise meal. Have this dish within 3 to 4 hours before your competition or training and you will be fuelled and ready to perform.

INGREDIENTS

150g egg noodles
1 tsp sesame oil
2 tbsp olive oil
½ a small onion, peeled and chopped
1 clove of garlic, peeled and chopped
½ a thumb-size piece of fresh ginger
a pinch of sea salt
3 free range chicken breast fillets, cut into strips
1 tbsp sweet chilli sauce
1 red pepper, deseeded and diced
2 tbsp soy sauce

PREPARATION

1. Boil 400ml of salted water in a medium-sized saucepan. Add the noodles and cook for 3 minutes or until they are almost cooked. Drain, rinse with cold water, toss with the sesame oil and set aside.
2. Add the olive oil to a frying pan over a medium heat. Add the onion, garlic, ginger and a pinch of salt. Cook for 1 to 2 minutes, stirring regularly.
3. Add the chicken strips, cook for 3 minutes then add the sweet chilli sauce and cook for another 2 to 3 minutes.
4. Add the diced pepper and soy sauce and mix well.
5. Add the noodles and toss gently. Cook for another 5 minutes, stirring well so that all the ingredients are thoroughly combined.
6. Serve in 2 shallow bowls.

Tips

- Swap the chicken for tofu to make this a meat-free option
- A high-carbohydrate meal to fuel performance

Fuel-up option

Greek Chicken Salad

SERVES	PREP TIME	CALORIES per serving (456g)	CARBS (g)	PROTEIN (g)	FAT (g)	FIBRE (g)
4	10 mins	500	11	45	26	4.8

 Rest Day Recipe

This Mediterranean-style salad is a classic, and for good reason. It's easily tossed together and is high in healthy fats from the olives, olive oil and cheese. The whopping 45g of protein it contains will keep you full all afternoon.

INGREDIENTS
1 tbsp olive oil
1 tsp dried oregano
sea salt and freshly ground
  black pepper
4 free range chicken breast
  mini fillets
4 tomatoes, chopped
1 cucumber, chopped
150g good-quality black
  olives, pitted
1 red onion, peeled and
  finely sliced
200g feta, cubed

For the dressing:
2 tbsp olive oil
1 tsp dried oregano
juice of 1 lemon
a pinch of sea salt and
  ground black pepper to
  your personal taste

PREPARATION
1. In a large bowl, mix the olive oil with the oregano, salt and pepper. Add the chicken and mix, ensuring it's well coated with the oil and herb mixture.
2. Place the chicken under a preheated grill and cook for 5 minutes each side.
3. In a large serving bowl, mix together the tomatoes, cucumber, olives, onion and feta.
4. Now make the dressing. Whisk all the ingredients together in a small bowl, then pour over the salad and toss well.
5. Divide the salad between four bowls and place the grilled mini fillets on top.

 Tips

- Excellent recovery meal option
- Quick and easy lunch option

Harissa Squash with Giant Couscous

SERVES	PREP TIME	COOKING TIME	CALORIES per serving (429g)	CARBS (g)	PROTEIN (g)	FAT (g)	FIBRE (g)
4	12 mins	30 mins	541	33	55	22	6.4

 Rest Day Recipe

Fancy a little spice in your food life? Then this one could be for you! Harissa is a Tunisian hot chilli pepper paste with roasted red peppers as the main ingredient. Harissa does an incredible job of bringing the squash and chicken to a new level.

INGREDIENTS

600g butternut squash, peeled and cubed
2 tbsp harissa paste
1 tsp olive oil
sea salt and freshly ground black pepper
4 free range chicken breast fillets
1 tsp olive oil
200g giant couscous
50g pumpkin seeds
2 handfuls of baby spinach leaves, washed
120g feta, crumbled

For the tahini dressing:
2 tbsp tahini
warm water
sea salt and freshly ground black pepper

PREPARATION

1. Preheat the oven to 180C°.
2. In a bowl, combine the squash, harissa paste, olive oil and salt and pepper.
3. Spread the squash out on a baking tray lined with greaseproof paper and roast for 25 to 30 minutes until soft. Allow to cool.
4. While the squash is in the oven, season the chicken and grill on both sides until cooked, about 15 minutes.
5. Pour the giant couscous into a pot of boiling water (about 400ml), cook for 7 to 8 minutes, then drain and allow to cool.
6. Next make the dressing by mixing the tahini with the salt and pepper in a small bowl. Gradually add warm water until it reaches a pourable consistency but is not too thin.
7. Dry fry the pumpkin seeds in a hot pan with some salt, shaking the pan regularly to ensure they don't burn.
8. In a large bowl, combine the squash, couscous, spinach leaves and feta.
9. Top with the pumpkin seeds and drizzle over the tahini dressing.
10. Divide between 4 plates, placing a grilled chicken breast on top of each one, and serve.

Hot and Sweet Chicken Stir-fry

SERVES	PREP TIME	COOKING TIME	CALORIES per serving (583g)	CARBS (g)	PROTEIN (g)	FAT (g)	FIBRE (g)
4	10 mins	20 mins	498	34	57	12	8.7

 Rest Day Recipe

A chicken stir-fry is one of the quickest and simplest meals you can put together. You can add a wide variety of vegetables to the recipe, which equates to (you guessed it) a wide variety of healthy nutrients. This chicken stir-fry is best suited to a day when you haven't been intensely active, but you can add a starchy carbohydrate like rice or noodles with it to easily turn it into a recovery meal.

INGREDIENTS

1 tbsp olive oil
1 onion, chopped
2 cloves of garlic, peeled and crushed
a thumb-sized piece of fresh ginger, grated
4 free range chicken breasts, chopped into chunks
3 carrots, thinly sliced
50g sugar snap peas
8 mushrooms, chopped
a small handful of cabbage, finely chopped or shredded
1 red pepper, deseeded and sliced
sea salt and freshly ground black pepper
1 red chilli, deseeded and chopped
juice of 1 grapefruit
2 tbsp honey
2 tbsp balsamic vinegar
2 tbsp olive oil

PREPARATION

1. Heat the olive oil in a large pan over a medium heat. Add the onion, garlic and ginger and sauté until softened and fragrant.
2. Add the chicken to the pan and cook for 3 to 4 minutes, stirring regularly
3. Next, add the sliced carrot, sugar snap peas, mushrooms, cabbage, pepper and chilli and continue to stir, keeping everything moving around the pan.
4. Mix the grapefruit juice, honey, vinegar and olive oil in a small dish. Once well mixed, pour over the stir-fry and cook for another 5 minutes.
5. Serve on its own or with rice or noodles on the side.

Tips

- Quick, simple and easy to put together, with great flavour
- Excellent protein source
- Great recipe to match with rice or noodles in preparation for competition
- Replace the chicken with chickpeas for a vegetarian option

Potato Bean Tuna Melt

SERVES	PREP TIME	COOKING TIME	CALORIES per serving (525g)	CARBS (g)	PROTEIN (g)	FAT (g)	FIBRE (g)
2	10 mins	50 mins	666	60	35	32	11

 Exercise Day Recipe

A little patience goes a long way. That can be said for this recipe as you will be glad you waited for your potatoes to bake slowly in the oven when you are layering your healthy toppings over them. This recipe offers plenty of carbohydrates to refuel and recover the body following exercise.

INGREDIENTS
2 medium potatoes, scrubbed
1 onion, peeled and chopped
1 tbsp olive oil
1 160g tin of tuna, drained
1 415g tin of baked beans
1 tbsp Greek yoghurt
1 tbsp chives, chopped
25g butter
sea salt and freshly ground black pepper
50g Cheddar cheese, grated

PREPARATION
1. Preheat the oven to 200°C.
2. Bake the potatoes in the hot oven until cooked through (about 50 minutes).
3. While the potatoes are cooking, fry the onion in the olive oil in a medium saucepan. When beginning to soften, add the tuna.
4. Heat the beans separately in a small saucepan, stirring regularly.
5. In a small bowl, mix the yoghurt and chives and add in the tuna and onion mix.
6. Remove the potatoes from the oven, put each on a plate and cut in half. Add butter, salt and pepper and mash through a little.
7. Pour the hot beans over the 4 potato halves, then divide the tuna, chive, yoghurt and onion mix between them. Top with the grated cheese and tuck in!

Tips

- Source of fast-releasing carbohydrate which enables a speedy recovery following exercise

Excellent protein source from the tuna

One-Pot Chicken and Spinach Pesto Pasta

SERVES	PREP TIME	COOKING TIME	CALORIES per serving (320g)	CARBS (g)	PROTEIN (g)	FAT (g)	FIBRE (g)
2	5 mins	20 mins	466	22	51	19	5

 Rest Day Recipe

One pot means a lot less washing up! All you need is the pot, the ingredients and you're ready to rumble. This recipe is easily digestible and low in fibre. If you want to increase the carbohydrate, simply add more spaghetti to the recipe.

INGREDIENTS

1 tbsp olive oil

1 onion, peeled and chopped

2 cloves of garlic, peeled and finely chopped

2 free range chicken breast fillets, chopped

a pinch of sea salt and freshly ground black pepper

8 mushrooms, chopped

150g spaghetti

a handful of baby spinach, washed

2 tbsp pesto*

50g Cheddar cheese, grated

PREPARATION

1. Boil a kettle of water and leave to cool slightly.
2. In a large saucepan (big enough to cook pasta in) heat the olive oil over a medium heat. Add the onions and garlic and fry for about 2 minutes, until softened.
3. Season the chicken with salt and pepper then add to the saucepan and cook for about 5 minutes, stirring frequently, until the chicken is almost cooked through.
4. Add the mushrooms and cook for another minute.
5. Pour 400ml of the water from the kettle into the saucepan then throw in your pasta.
6. Add the spinach and stir.
7. Cook for 5 minutes, stirring regularly so the pasta doesn't stick together.
8. The water should be almost absorbed at this point. Next stir in the pesto and cook for the remainder of the time it says on the pasta packet (probably another 5 minutes).
9. Serve with grated Cheddar cheese sprinkled over.

Bonus recipe

If you want to make your own pesto for this dish, here is a quick and simple recipe:

Ingredients

4 small bunches of fresh basil leaves

1 clove of garlic, peeled

2 tbsp pine nuts, lightly toasted in a dry frying pan

2 tbsp Parmesan cheese, grated

2 tbsp extra virgin olive oil

a pinch of black and white pepper

Preparation

1. Put all the ingredients in a blender and whizz to a smooth paste.
2. Store in the fridge for up to a week to use at will!

Prawn Stir-Fry

SERVES	PREP TIME	COOKING TIME	CALORIES per serving (476g)	CARBS (g)	PROTEIN (g)	FAT (g)	FIBRE (g)
2	10 mins	10 mins	390	53	32	6	9.4

 Exercise Day Recipe

Everyone should have this recipe in their armoury, if just for a nutritious meal.
It's easily whipped up in a jiffy for an ideal fuel-up recipe. It also works well as a quick
post-workout recovery meal. If you're not a fish lover, no problem! Switch out the prawns
for chicken if you prefer.

INGREDIENTS
1 tbsp coconut oil
1 chilli, deseeded and finely
  sliced
2 cloves of garlic, peeled
  and crushed
a thumb-size piece of fresh
  ginger, peeled and grated
1 red pepper, deseeded and
  thinly sliced
a small head of broccoli,
  chopped into small florets
200g raw, peeled king
  prawns
2 tbsp soy sauce
1 tbsp sweet chilli sauce
1 300g pack of straight to
wok rice noodles*

PREPARATION
1. Heat the coconut oil in a wok and add the chilli, garlic and ginger. Cook until it becomes fragrant, making sure it doesn't burn.
2. Quickly add the pepper and broccoli and stir-fry for 5 to 6 minutes.
3. Next add the prawns and cook until they turn pink, about 3 to 4 minutes.
4. Pour over the soy sauce and sweet chilli sauce and mix well, making sure the vegetables and prawns are well coated.
5. Add the noodles to the wok, heat through and combine well. Divide between two bowls and enjoy.

* *If you don't have straight to wok noodles, cook dry noodles separately in a pot of boiling water for 4 to 5 minutes. Drain. Then combine with the prawns and vegetables at Step 5.*

Tips

- A high-carbohydrate meal to fuel performance or recover and refuel following exercise
- The broccoli provides a rich source of vitamin C

Quinoa Salmon Salad

SERVES	PREP TIME	COOKING TIME	CALORIES per serving (476g)	CARBS (g)	PROTEIN (g)	FAT (g)	FIBRE (g)
2	10 mins	30 mins	596	13	34	46	7.2

 Rest Day Recipe

This salad offers a range of healthy vitamins and trace minerals to boost your immune system. It's packed full of healthy fats such as omega-3 (which comes from the salmon). Salmon plays a double role in this salad as it also provides a great protein hit.

INGREDIENTS

50g quinoa
2 tbsp olive oil
2 salmon fillets, preferably wild or organic
75g baby spinach, washed
½ a cucumber, chopped
1 ripe avocado, flesh chopped
1 red pepper, deseeded and diced
25g pumpkin seeds, toasted in a dry pan
sea salt and freshly ground black pepper
1 tbsp lemon juice

PREPARATION

1. Rinse the quinoa under cold water. Put into a saucepan and add double the amount of water (about 200ml).
Add a pinch of salt and bring to a boil. Reduce the heat and simmer for 10 to 15 minutes or until the liquid has been absorbed.

2. Meanwhile, heat 1 tbsp of olive oil in a pan. Add the salmon fillets to the hot pan, flesh side down. Cook for 4 to 5 minutes, then turn and cook for a further 4 to 5 minutes. Once cooked, flake the salmon and set aside.

3. In a large bowl, mix together the quinoa, spinach, cucumber, avocado and red pepper.

4. Arrange the flaked salmon over the top of the salad and sprinkle with the toasted pumpkin seeds.

5. Season with salt and pepper and drizzle with the remaining 1 tbsp of olive oil and the lemon juice.

Tips

- Low-carbohydrate meal with a good source of healthy fats and protein
- Provides all of your daily required amount of omega-3

Provides a healthy source of vitamins D, E and K

Quinoa Super Salad

SERVES	PREP TIME	COOKING TIME	CALORIES per serving (343g)	CARBS (g)	PROTEIN (g)	FAT (g)	FIBRE (g)
4	10 mins	20 mins	526	37	23	34	9.7

 Exercise Day Recipe

Why super? Because this quinoa salad is packed with flavour and high in slow-digesting energy. Quinoa is an ancient grain – mainly unchanged from what our ancestors ate. It is naturally gluten-free and is rich in protein, plus it has a low glycaemic index. This salad works well as a side option or as an alternative to pasta and rice if you're looking for some variety.

INGREDIENTS

1 tbsp rapeseed oil
1 red onion, peeled and
  finely chopped
2 cloves of garlic, peeled
  and finely chopped
200g quinoa (rinsed)
250ml water
1 tsp ground turmeric
a pinch of sea salt
1 tsp cumin seeds
5 tbsp sesame seeds
5 tbsp sunflower seeds
4 tbsp pumpkin seeds
200g tinned chickpeas,
  drained and rinsed
2 tbsp dried cranberries
3 sprigs of fresh coriander,
  roughly chopped
sea salt and freshly ground
  black pepper

PREPARATION

1. Heat the oil in a pan over a medium heat. Add the onion and garlic and fry for 5 minutes, stirring occasionally. Add the quinoa and cook on a low heat for 1 minute. Add the water, turmeric and a pinch of salt and bring to the boil, then reduce the heat and simmer for 15 minutes, until the quinoa is cooked through and the water has been absorbed.
2. Meanwhile, set a dry frying pan over a low heat. Toast the cumin, sesame, sunflower and pumpkin seeds for 6 minutes, tossing regularly, until fragrant.
3. Transfer the cooked quinoa mixture to a large salad bowl and fluff up with a fork before stirring in the toasted seeds and the chickpeas, cranberries and fresh coriander.
4. Season with a pinch of salt and pepper and serve straight away or refrigerate to eat later as a cold salad.

Add some rocket or baby kale leaves into this dish at Step 3 if you want to get some antioxidant-rich healthy greens into your diet.

Tips

- Healthy fats come from the sesame, sunflower and pumpkin seeds
- Provides many required trace minerals such as iron, magnesium, zinc and copper

Spicy Chicken Tenders with Roast Sweet Potato

SERVES	PREP TIME	COOKING TIME	CALORIES per serving (301g)	CARBS (g)	PROTEIN (g)	FAT (g)	FIBRE (g)
3	10 mins	40 mins	567	13	69	27	1.9

 Rest Day Recipe

Try this recipe on for size and experience the appetising flavour of spicy chicken tenders with crunchy roast sweet potato. This meal works great for either lunch or an evening meal after a long day and packs a whopping amount of protein and flavour.

INGREDIENTS
2 sweet potatoes, cut into wedges
1 tbsp olive oil
½ tsp smoked paprika
salt and pepper
2 tbsp honey
1 tbsp chilli flakes
½ tsp black pepper
1 tsp garlic powder
a pinch of sea salt
12 strips bacon or pancetta, sliced in half
4 free range chicken breasts, each cut lengthwise into 3 tenders

PREPARATION
1. Preheat the oven to 200°C.
2. Put the sweet potato wedges in a bowl and toss with the olive oil, smoked paprika and a pinch of salt and pepper. Spread out on a baking tray lined with greaseproof paper and roast in the oven for 40 minutes, until cooked through and crisp.
3. Meanwhile, prepare the chicken tenders. Mix the honey, paprika, chilli flakes, black pepper, garlic powder and salt in a small dish.
4. Wrap 2 bacon strips around each chicken tender and pin together with a cocktail stick.
5. Drizzle the chilli-honey mixture evenly over the chicken tenders, completely coating them.
6. Sauté the bacon-wrapped tenders in a little oil in a non-stick frying pan for 5 minutes.
7. Transfer into the oven and bake for 20 minutes or until cooked through.
8. Serve with the roast sweet potatoes.

 Tips

- Low-carbohydrate meal with some slow-releasing energy from the sweet potato

Big hit of protein

Roasted Vegetable Salad with Hummus

SERVES	PREP TIME	COOKING TIME	CALORIES per serving (538g)	CARBS (g)	PROTEIN (g)	FAT (g)	FIBRE (g)
4	15 mins	20-25 mins	526	23	25	39	11

 Rest Day Recipe

This is a lovely warm salad with an array of flavours that combine brilliantly with the melting feta cheese and steaming-hot courgettes. It certainly packs its weight in nutritional value with healthy fat from the hummus and feta cheese and plant-based protein from quinoa and hummus. Enjoy as a work lunch, starter or side dish.

INGREDIENTS

3 peppers, different colours, deseeded and sliced
2 courgettes, chopped
olive oil
sea salt and freshly ground black pepper
2 tbsp hazelnuts
120g quinoa
200g hummus (bought or homemade, see p. 171)
4 tbsp pesto (bought or homemade, see p. 127)
200g feta

PREPARATION

1. Preheat the oven to 170°C.
2. Arrange the peppers and courgettes on a baking tray lined with greaseproof paper, toss with olive oil, salt and pepper and bake in the oven for 12 to 15 minutes until tender.
3. Put the hazelnuts on a small baking tray and place in the hot oven for 6 minutes, watching them carefully so they don't burn.
4. Meanwhile put the quinoa in a saucepan and pour in double the amount of salted water. Bring to the boil, cover and simmer for 10 to 15 minutes, until the quinoa is soft and all the water has been absorbed.
5. In a large salad bowl, mix the quinoa, nuts and roasted veg together, being sure to pour in any remaining tasty olive oil from the baking tray.
6. Divide between 4 plates and top each portion with a serving of hummus and pesto. Finish by crumbling the feta over the top.

Tips

- Offers an array of healthy fats
- Best to use as a side dish or for a low-intensity exercise day

Ancient Grain Mixed Seed Salad

SERVES	PREP TIME	COOKING TIME	CALORIES per serving (270g)	CARBS (g)	PROTEIN (g)	FAT (g)	FIBRE (g)
2	10 mins	12 mins	650	66	25	33	17

 Exercise Day Recipe

This salad is packed with flavour and rich in carbohydrates and works well as a side to a main meal as an alternative to pasta or rice if you are looking for some variety. Quinoa is the ancient grain in the title and has high nutrition benefits. As a snack, it works well on carb-loading days and works well in a lunch box to grab on your way to work.

INGREDIENTS
1 tbsp coconut oil
1 onion, peeled and finely chopped
2 cloves of garlic, peeled and finely chopped
½ a thumb-size piece of fresh ginger, peeled and grated
180g quinoa, rinsed
250ml water
1 tsp turmeric
a pinch of sea salt
5 tbsp sunflower seeds
5 tbsp sesame seeds
1 tsp cumin seeds
240g tinned chickpeas, drained
1 small carrot, grated
10 cherry tomatoes, cut into quarters
a handful of fresh coriander, roughly chopped

PREPARATION
1. In a large saucepan, fry the onion, garlic and ginger in the coconut oil over a medium heat for 5 minutes, stirring occasionally.
2. Stir in the quinoa, then lower the heat and cook for 1 minute.
3. Pour in the water and add the turmeric and a pinch of salt. Bring to the boil then simmer for 15 minutes.
4. Toast the sunflower, sesame and cumin seeds in a dry frying pan for 6 minutes, shaking the pan to make sure they're evenly done.
5. Now it's time to assemble your salad. Get a big salad bowl and add the quinoa, toasted seeds, chickpeas, grated carrot, tomatoes, and fresh coriander. Mix gently before serving. You can store it in the fridge for a few days if you want to use it for packed lunches.

Tips

- **High-carbohydrate meal to fuel the body for exercise**
- **Super plant-based protein meal**

Spicy Baked Eggs with Beans

SERVES	PREP TIME	COOKING TIME	CALORIES per serving (570g)	CARBS (g)	PROTEIN (g)	FAT (g)	FIBRE (g)
3	5 mins	5 mins	523	25	49	27	5.2

 Rest Day Recipe

Hugely filling and satisfying! This baked eggs and beans dish is ideal for a non-training day breakfast, lunch or dinner. It is high in protein and healthy fats and the beans and vegetables provide loads of fibre. Make it vegetarian by leaving out the mince.

INGREDIENTS

1 tbsp olive oil
300g lean beef mince
1 onion, peeled and
  chopped
a small head of broccoli,
  chopped finely
1 red chilli, deseeded and
  finely chopped
6 mushrooms, chopped
1 415g tin of baked beans,
  rinsed and drained
1 400g tin of chopped
  tomatoes
4 free range eggs
sea salt and freshly ground
  black pepper
mature Cheddar cheese,
  grated, or mozzarella,
  chopped

PREPARATION

1. Preheat the oven to 200°C.
2. Brown the beef in the olive oil in a large, oven-proof pan on a medium heat.
3. Add the onion, broccoli, chilli and mushrooms, and continue to cook for 5 minutes, stirring regularly.
4. Add the beans and chopped tomatoes, and stir for 2 minutes.
5. Create 4 wells in the mix, and carefully crack an egg into each well.
6. Season with salt and pepper and bake in the oven for 5 minutes.
7. Remove and sprinkle the Cheddar or mozzarella on top and bake for a further 5 minutes until the cheese is melted and bubbling.

Tips

- **Big hit of protein**
- **Very filling lunch or dinner**
- **Rest day meal**

Spicy Prawn Noodle Salad

SERVES	PREP TIME	COOKING TIME	CALORIES per serving (467g)	CARBS (g)	PROTEIN (g)	FAT (g)	FIBRE (g)
2	5 mins	10 mins	502	39	26	28	8.3

 Exercise Day Recipe

Searching for something that's simple to cook, easy to digest and tastes amazing? Bingo! You've selected the perfect recipe. The spicy prawn noodle salad is served fresh, hot and ready to go. If you are tight for time, then whip this up in a flash and you'll be delighted with how good it tastes.

INGREDIENTS

200g noodles
1 tbsp sesame oil
3 spring onions, sliced
1 red chilli, deseeded and diced
100g mangetout
100g baby corn, halved lengthways
1 red pepper, deseeded and sliced thinly
200g cooked prawns
a handful of fresh coriander, chopped

For the dressing:

2 tbsp olive oil
1 tbsp sesame oil
2 tbsp soy sauce
juice of 1 lime
1 tsp honey

PREPARATION

1. Cook the noodles in boiling salted water for the amount of time it says on the packet. Drain, rinse with cold water and set aside.
2. Heat the sesame oil in a pan over a medium heat and stir-fry the spring onions, chilli, prawns, mangetout, corn and pepper for 4 to 5 minutes. Be careful not to overcook the veg – they should still have some 'bite'. Set aside.
3. Combine the sautéed vegetables and prawns with the noodles in a large bowl and mix through the chopped coriander.
4. Put all the ingredients for the dressing in a small bowl or clean jam jar and mix/shake. Pour the dressing over the salad, toss and serve.

Tips

- Simple, quick to cook and tastes great
- Can be used as a pre-competition fuel-up option if you drop the chilli and reduce the portion of vegetables
- Great fuel-up or recovery meal option
- For a vegetarian alternative, replace the prawns with tofu or a tin of chickpeas

Turkey Burgers

SERVES	PREP TIME	COOKING TIME	CALORIES per serving (232g)	CARBS (g)	PROTEIN (g)	FAT (g)	FIBRE (g)
4	10 mins	25 mins	273	4	39	11	1

 Rest Day Recipe

We often associate turkey with the festive season, but it is actually a hugely versatile white meat that can be enjoyed any time of the year. Turkey mince is readily available and these burgers can be whipped up very quickly in one bowl. Turkey meat is a lean source of protein, making it ideal for those looking for higher-protein food options.

INGREDIENTS

600g turkey mince
1 free range egg, beaten
2 tbsp extra virgin olive oil
½ a red onion, peeled and
    finely chopped
100g courgette, grated
1 tsp ground cumin
2 large garlic cloves,
    peeled and finely
    chopped
1 tsp ground ginger
½ tsp paprika
1 tbsp tomato purée
zest of ½ a lime
a sprinkle of dried mixed
    herbs
sea salt and freshly ground
    black pepper

PREPARATION

1. Preheat the oven to 180°C.
2. Put all the ingredients into a large bowl. Using clean hands, mix and squish everything together.
3. Grab handfuls of the mixture and form into 4 to 6 burgers – start with a ball then flatten and pat with your hands into a burger shape.
4. Place the burgers on a plate and drizzle with a touch of olive oil. Tip: If you want to make these in advance, you could refrigerate them, covered, at this point for a few hours.
5. Fry the burgers in a hot non-stick pan for a minute on each side to lock in the flavour and give some colour, then transfer to a baking sheet and put in the oven for 20 minutes.
6. Serve with some sweet potato wedges, roasted with ½ tsp each of salt, cumin and paprika (see also page 133).

Tips

- **Low-carbohydrate meal**
- **Packs a huge amount of protein**
- **Very satisfying and filling meal**

Whip Up Tuna Stir-fry

SERVES	PREP TIME	COOKING TIME	CALORIES per serving (704g)	CARBS (g)	PROTEIN (g)	FAT (g)	FIBRE (g)
1	5 mins	15 mins	514	27	47	23	8.1

 Rest Day Recipe

A get-out-of-jail recipe! This is perfect for those times when you are late or in a rush and want something healthy but really quick and easy to make. A handy tin of tuna is a great source of protein and combined with some stir-fry veg makes for a healthy and satisfying dish.

INGREDIENTS

1 tbsp coconut oil
1 medium red onion, peeled and chopped
1 clove of garlic, peeled and crushed
1 large bell pepper, deseeded and chopped
8 mushrooms, chopped
1 tbsp soy sauce
a handful of baby spinach, washed
a pinch of sea salt and freshly ground black pepper
1 160g tin of tuna, drained
grated Parmesan or Cheddar cheese, to finish

PREPARATION

1. Heat the coconut oil in a medium-sized pan over a medium heat. Add the onion, garlic, pepper and mushrooms and stir well. Drizzle over the soy sauce.
2. Stir-fry all the vegetables until they start to take on some colour, then add in the spinach and cook for another 2 to 3 minutes, until the spinach is wilted. Season with salt and pepper as you cook.
3. Lastly, add in your tuna, mix through the veg and season again.
4. Add a little Parmesan or grated Cheddar cheese on top for extra flavour before serving.

Excellent recovery meal option

DINNER

Aubergine Lasagne

SERVES	PREP TIME	COOKING TIME	CALORIES per serving (700g)	CARBS (g)	PROTEIN (g)	FAT (g)	FIBRE (g)
2	15 mins	1 hour	667	22	49	39	9

 Rest Day Recipe

This classic dish transforms into a low-carb option by using aubergine and greens instead of pasta to layer. The addition of vegetables also makes it higher in fibre than its pasta-based cousin. Make sure you buy firm, glossy aubergines for the best flavour.

INGREDIENTS

9 large tomatoes
a splash of red wine
3 tbsp crème fraîche
1 tbsp fresh basil, chopped
1 tbsp dried oregano
½ tsp paprika
4 large cloves of garlic, crushed
1 medium onion, peeled and diced
sea salt and freshly ground
   black pepper

1 tbsp tomato purée
2 tbsp olive oil
500g lean minced beef
2 tbsp Worcestershire sauce
1 red pepper, deseeded
   and chopped
1 yellow pepper, deseeded
   and chopped
2 large aubergines, sliced as
   thinly as possible
olive oil, for brushing

4 giant collard green leaves,
   stems removed (spinach
   can also be used)
10 button mushrooms, sliced
1 tbsp tomato purée
1 large ball fresh
   mozzarella, grated
Cheddar cheese, grated
   (optional)

PREPARATION

For the tomato sauce:

1. Blend the whole tomatoes with the red wine, crème fraîche, basil, oregano, paprika, garlic, onion, salt, pepper and tomato purée.

2. In a large pan, heat 1 tbsp of the olive oil over a medium heat. Add the beef and the Worcestershire sauce and cook for 5 to 10 minutes until slightly brown. Once nearly cooked, add the chopped peppers.

3. Pour in the tomato sauce – reserving some for the final layer – and stir through the beef. Cover and simmer gently for 15 minutes.

For the lasagne:

1. Preheat the oven to 190°C. Grease a glass oven-proof dish with coconut oil.

2. Brush the aubergine slices with olive oil and season both sides with salt and pepper. Make a single layer on the bottom of the dish using a third of the aubergine.

3. Layer half the collard greens/spinach leaves over the aubergine slices.

4. Divide the meat sauce mixture in half and spoon over the collard greens.

5. Top with half of the mushroom slices.

6. Create another layer: aubergine, greens, meat sauce and mushrooms.

7. Top the final layer with the remaining aubergine slices and spread over the reserved tomato sauce.

8. Scatter the mozzarella cheese (and Cheddar if you like it cheesy) on top.

9. Bake for 40 minutes and cut into squares to serve.

Beef Bolognese with Carrot 'Pasta'

SERVES	PREP TIME	COOKING TIME	CALORIES per serving (940g)	CARBS (g)	PROTEIN (g)	FAT (g)	FIBRE (g)
2/3	15 mins	20 mins	658	34	63	30	14

 Rest Day Recipe

This meal packs a massive 63g of protein per serving, which is a big hit!
My athletes love to eat this in the off-season as it's a tasty and nutritious meal but avoids the carb intensity of pasta.

INGREDIENTS

2 tbsp olive oil
2 cloves of garlic, peeled and chopped
500g lean minced beef
a pinch of sea salt
½ a leek, washed and chopped
½ a white onion, peeled and chopped
½ a red onion, peeled and chopped

freshly ground black pepper
½ a red pepper, deseeded and chopped
½ a green pepper, deseeded and chopped
½ a yellow pepper, deseeded and chopped
chilli flakes
1 400g tin of chopped tomatoes
2 tbsp tomato purée

10 fresh basil leaves
a handful of fresh coriander, chopped
3 carrots, peeled and spiralised or sliced lengthwise into very thin strips
Parmesan cheese, grated (optional)

PREPARATION

1. Heat the olive oil in a large saucepan over a medium heat. Add the garlic and cook for 2 minutes. Add the beef and a pinch of salt and cook until just a little pink remains.
2. Add in the leek, onions, peppers, chilli flakes and freshly ground black pepper. Simmer for 8–10 minutes.
3. Add in the chopped tomatoes, tomato purée and fresh herbs and cook for another 5 minutes.
4. Steam the spiralised or sliced carrots for 3 to 4 minutes unit soft but not soggy. Remove any water then place on a plate.
5. Serve the carrot 'pasta' in bowls with the beef and vegetable Bolognese on top.
6. Sprinkle some grated Parmesan on top for extra flavour.

Beef and Broccoli Stir-Fry

SERVES	PREP TIME	COOKING TIME	CALORIES per serving (466g)	CARBS (g)	PROTEIN (g)	FAT (g)	FIBRE (g)
2	5 mins	10 – 12 mins	353	23	26	19	11

 Rest Day Recipe

With a good balance of carbs, protein, and fat, this stir-fry is a dish that satisfies an active lifestyle. Broccoli provides an excellent source of vitamin K, which has proven immune-boosting powers. Enjoy this meal with or without rice, depending on your level of physical activity.

INGREDIENTS

1 tsp honey
1 tsp sesame oil
1 tbsp soy sauce
1 tbsp olive oil
1 clove of garlic, crushed
1 medium onion, peeled and sliced
1 small head of broccoli, chopped
2 medium carrots, thinly sliced
1 red pepper, deseeded and sliced
6 mushrooms, chopped
1 medium-sized sirloin steak, cut into strips
a pinch of sea salt

PREPARATION

1. In a small dish mix the honey with the sesame oil and soy sauce. Set aside.
2. Heat the olive oil in a large skillet, add the garlic and onion and sauté for a minute. Add in the broccoli, carrots, pepper and mushrooms.
3. Cook, stirring regularly, until the veggies are crisp but tender and onions are browned.
4. Add in the beef strips and the sauce mixed earlier, increase the heat and cook to your desired level – rare, medium or well done. Season with a pinch of salt.
5. Serve on a bed of white or brown rice. If you're in a hurry, use boil-in-the-bag rice.

Tips

- Contains moderate calories and is reasonably balanced across all macronutrients
- A balanced meal, ideal for an active lifestyle
- High in vitamin K, vitamin A and vitamin C with immune-boosting properties
- For a meat-free option, substitute the beef with tofu or beans

Burrito Bowl

SERVES	PREP TIME	COOKING TIME	CALORIES per serving (907g)	CARBS (g)	PROTEIN (g)	FAT (g)	FIBRE (g)
3	10 mins	25 mins	733	100	35	23	33

 Exercise Day Recipe

Impress your friends or a special someone with this storm of a Mexican burrito bowl! Not only is it delicious, it's also a perfect post-exercise meal as the high carbs replenish your fuel stores.

INGREDIENTS

3 tbsp olive oil
2 carrots, chopped
2 sweet potatoes, roughly chopped
1 onion, peeled and chopped
1 clove of garlic, peeled and chopped
10 mushrooms, chopped
1 red pepper, deseeded and chopped
1 yellow pepper, deseeded and chopped

150g quinoa
1 400g tin of chickpeas
1 400g tin of black beans
100g frozen peas
juice of 1 lemon
a handful of fresh coriander, chopped
8 cherry tomatoes, chopped
100g feta cheese

For the dressing:
½ tsp ground turmeric
1 tsp curry powder
a drizzle of honey
100g Greek yoghurt

For the guacamole:
1 tbsp olive oil
1 ripe avocado
juice of 1 lemon
sea salt and freshly ground black pepper

PREPARATION

1. Preheat the oven to 200°C.
2. Place the carrot and sweet potato on a baking tray lined with greaseproof paper, drizzle with a little oil and roast in the oven for 20 minutes.
3. Heat 1 tbsp oil in a saucepan on a medium heat and sauté the onions, garlic, mushrooms and peppers until soft.
4. Cook the quinoa in twice its volume of boiling water for 12 minutes until the water has evaporated and the quinoa is tender.
5. Meanwhile, gently warm the chickpeas, black beans and peas in a pot with the lemon juice and chopped coriander.
6. Make the dressing by mixing the turmeric, curry powder and honey with the yoghurt.
7. For the guacamole, simply mash the avocado with a little olive oil and lemon juice. Season with salt and pepper.
8. Put the cooked quinoa in a medium-sized bowl to create a bed for the rest of the ingredients. Next add the roasted sweet potato and carrot, then the beans and peas, followed by the sautéed veg and chopped tomatoes.
9. Top the dish with the guacamole, yoghurt curry dressing and a crumbling of feta cheese.

Cauliflower Carbonara

SERVES	PREP TIME	COOKING TIME	CALORIES per serving (317g)	CARBS (g)	PROTEIN (g)	FAT (g)	FIBRE (g)
2	5 mins	20 mins	431	10	30	30	1.1

 Rest Day Recipe

This dish is just delicious and surprisingly easy and quick to make. I can't take credit for it, though, as this is my mammy's recipe. She is a genius at coming up with simple but clever dishes with great taste. This low-carbohydrate recipe can be enjoyed on its own or would go perfectly as a side with chicken or fish.

INGREDIENTS

1 head of cauliflower, chopped into florets
1 tbsp olive oil
3 tbsp lean bacon, chopped into pieces
300ml whole milk
2 free range egg yolks
2 tbsp Greek yoghurt
100g Cheddar cheese
sea salt and freshly ground black pepper to taste

PREPARATION

1. Boil or steam the cauliflower for 5 minutes.
2. Heat the oil and fry the bacon in a large saucepan for 2 to 3 minutes until crisping up.
3. In a small dish, whisk the milk with the egg yolks, salt and pepper and pour into the saucepan with the bacon.
4. Add the cauliflower and Greek yoghurt and mix well until the cauliflower is completely coated.
5. Pour the mix into an oven-proof glass dish, spread out evenly and grate the Cheddar cheese over the top.
6. Place the dish under the grill for 5 to 7 minutes until the top turns brown and the cheese is bubbling.

 Tips

• **Makes a wonderful side dish with chicken**

Low-carbohydrate option

Action-Packed Chicken Broccoli Bake

SERVES	PREP TIME	COOKING TIME	CALORIES per serving (455g)	CARBS (g)	PROTEIN (g)	FAT (g)	FIBRE (g)
4	10 mins	25 mins	601	16	53	36	6.4

 Rest Day Recipe

Read down the list of ingredients and you'll see why I've called this healthy twist on a classic comfort dish 'action-packed'! It's high in protein while providing a moderate portion of carbohydrate. If you're seeking a high-energy, comforting, tasty meal and have worked up an appetite, look no further.

INGREDIENTS

100g quinoa
2 tbsp olive oil
1 white onion, peeled and diced
3 cloves of garlic, peeled and crushed
a pinch of sea salt
4 free range chicken breasts, chopped
½ tbsp dried oregano
½ tbsp dried coriander
1 red pepper, chopped
8 mushrooms, chopped
1 large head of broccoli, chopped
1 400g tin of chopped tomatoes
1 400ml tin of coconut milk
2 handfuls of fresh spinach, washed
1 red onion, peeled and diced
70g reduced-fat Cheddar cheese, grated

PREPARATION

1. Preheat the oven to 200°C.
2. Boil the quinoa in 250ml salted water until cooked (add half a stock cube or ½ tsp Marigold powder for more flavour).
3. Heat the oil in a large pan over a medium heat. Add the onion and garlic with a little salt, and cook for 2 to 3 minutes until the onion starts to turn brown.
4. Add the chopped chicken, oregano and coriander, stir well and cook for 5 minutes.
5. Add the chopped peppers and mushrooms, cook for 3 to 4 minutes, then tip in the chopped tomatoes and mix well.
6. When the vegetables and chicken are almost cooked, pour in the coconut milk. When that begins to simmer, stir in the cooked quinoa.
7. Add the spinach and let it wilt down.
8. Now it's time to assemble your bake. Transfer the mixture into a casserole dish, spread out evenly, then sprinkle the chopped broccoli and red onion over it. Finish with some Cheddar cheese.
9. Bake in the oven for 10 to 15 minutes until the broccoli begins to turn brown and the cheese is melted.
10. Remove from the oven and serve warm.

Tips

- **Rich source of fibre**
- **Low-carbohydrate dinner option**

Chicken and Vegetable Pie

SERVES	PREP TIME	COOKING TIME	CALORIES per serving (793g)	CARBS (g)	PROTEIN (g)	FAT (g)	FIBRE (g)
3	10 mins	35 mins	760	50	68	34	16

 Exercise Day Recipe

High-protein meals post-workout are important for muscle recovery and repair and this dinner packs a whopping 68g! The fact that it's also low in carbs and high in nutrients from the veg make it a perfect recovery option. It's also a great choice for a sit-down family meal.

INGREDIENTS

1 tbsp olive oil
2 cloves of garlic, peeled and crushed
1 onion, peeled and chopped
500g free range chicken breast, chopped
10 mushrooms, sliced
2 sticks celery, sliced
1 red pepper, deseeded and chopped
1 yellow pepper, deseeded and chopped
1 head of broccoli, chopped
3 tbsp frozen garden peas
sea salt and freshly ground black pepper
a pinch of ground nutmeg
a bunch of fresh flat-leaf parsley, finely chopped
1 250ml carton of coconut cream
400g potatoes, peeled and cut into chunks
2 large carrots, peeled and cut into chunks
butter, for mashing
100g Cheddar cheese, grated

PREPARATION

1. Preheat the oven to 180°C.
2. First heat the olive oil in a saucepan, add the garlic and onion and fry for 2 to 3 minutes until softened. Stir in the chopped chicken.
3. Add the mushrooms, celery, peppers, broccoli and peas to the pan with the chicken and season with the salt, pepper and nutmeg and parsley.
4. Gradually add the coconut cream, stir and allow to simmer for 5 minutes.
5. Place the potatoes and carrots in a steamer and cook for 20 minutes or until soft.
6. Remove the potato and carrots and put them in a saucepan with a little butter and salt, then mash.
7. Transfer the chicken and vegetables into a casserole dish. Next spoon the mashed potato and carrot over the top and spread out evenly.
8. Top with a little grated cheese then bake in the oven for 15 minutes until the crust is golden brown.

Tips

- **Excellent source of protein**
- **Great recovery meal after training or an intense workout**
- **Hugely satisfying**

Chicken Korma with Cauliflower Rice

SERVES	PREP TIME	COOKING TIME	CALORIES per serving (376g)	CARBS (g)	PROTEIN (g)	FAT (g)	FIBRE (g)
3	10 mins	50 mins	672	22	47	44	6

 Rest Day Recipe

You can serve this with traditional rice but try this alternative. It is a great way of reducing both the calories and the carbohydrate level of a meal without compromising on flavour. It may take a little longer than other recipes to cook, but the final results are worth the wait.

INGREDIENTS

3 free range chicken breasts, chopped
2 tbsp extra virgin olive oil
2 cloves of garlic, peeled and crushed
2 tsp curry powder
½ tsp sea salt
½ tsp freshly ground black pepper
1 red chilli, deseeded and diced
1 onion, peeled and finely chopped

For the korma sauce:

2 onions, peeled and chopped
3 cloves of garlic, peeled and crushed
½ a small red chilli, deseeded and chopped
½ a small green chilli, deseeded and chopped
2 tsp curry powder
1 tsp ground turmeric
1 tsp ground cinnamon
a small handful of fresh coriander, finely chopped
1 tsp sea salt
1 tsp freshly ground black pepper
½ tsp ground cumin

a thumb-sized piece of fresh ginger, grated
1 250ml carton of coconut cream
2 tbsp Greek yoghurt
1 tbsp honey

For the cauliflower rice:

1 head of cauliflower, leaves and stalk removed, florets cut into pieces
1 tbsp olive oil
1 tsp sea salt
½ tsp black pepper
1 tsp chilli powder
20g fresh coriander, chopped (optional)

PREPARATION

1. Marinate the chicken with 1 tbsp olive oil, a clove of garlic, the curry powder, salt and pepper for at least 2 hours or overnight.
2. When you are ready to cook, heat 1 tbsp of olive oil in a large pan and sauté the remaining garlic, the chilli and onion for 2 to 3 minutes until the onion begins to brown.
3. Add in the chicken and cook, stirring regularly, for about 10 minutes.
4. Meanwhile, make the korma sauce: place the onions, garlic, chillies and a little water in a blender and blitz to a creamy texture.
5. Measure out the spices (curry powder through cumin) into a small bowl.
6. Add the korma to the chicken mix and cook for 2 to 3 minutes, stirring constantly.

7. Add the ginger, coconut cream, yoghurt, pre-measured spices and honey and mix together.

8. Turn the heat down to low and simmer for 35 to 40 minutes, stirring regularly, until the sauce has reduced.

9. While this is cooking blitz the cauliflower florets in a food processor or blender until it's the size and texture of rice. Remove any larger pieces.

10. Heat the olive oil in a non-stick frying pan, add the cauliflower and spread out evenly. Next add the salt, pepper, chilli and any other spices of choice.

11. Keep stirring the cauliflower until it becomes light, fluffy and dry. Remove the cauliflower once you notice the edges becoming slightly brown but make sure not to burn – it only takes 5 to 6 minutes. Serve with the piping hot chicken korma, scattering on some fresh coriander if you like.

- To change this to an excersise day recipe, simply serve with white rice

Chilli Con Carne

SERVES	PREP TIME	COOKING TIME	CALORIES per serving (690g)	CARBS (g)	PROTEIN (g)	FAT (g)	FIBRE (g)
3	10 mins	35 mins	520	35	50	20	20

 Rest Day Recipe

This legendary crowd-pleaser is a meal best served piping hot; for an added bonus I've included chillies, cumin and cinnamon, sources of antioxidants. Due to the high amount of fibre from the veg and beans, I advise that you wait until after your workout for this one. Sit back and take your time to savour the delicious combination of flavours.

INGREDIENTS

2 tbsp olive oil
1 onion, finely diced
3 red chillies, deseeded and finely sliced (leave the seeds in if you like spice)
2 cloves of garlic, peeled and crushed
2 red peppers, deseeded and chopped
500g lean minced beef
2 tbsp ground cumin
1 tbsp ground cinnamon
1 tbsp paprika
1 400g tin of chopped tomatoes
juice of 1 lime
1 400g tin of kidney beans, drained
a handful of fresh coriander, chopped
1 tbsp honey
strong Cheddar, grated, and shredded iceberg lettuce to serve

PREPARATION

1. In a large saucepan over a medium heat, sauté the onion in the oil for 10 minutes before adding the chillies, garlic and peppers.
2. Add in the meat and the cumin, cinnamon and paprika.
3. Cook until the meat is brown, keeping it moving around the pan constantly, then add in the chopped tomatoes.
4. Simmer gently, uncovered, for 20 minutes.
5. Add in the lime juice and kidney beans, and simmer for another 5 minutes.
6. Stir in fresh coriander and honey to taste. If you like it even spicier, add either cayenne pepper or dried chilli flakes.
7. Serve with brown rice, guacamole (see p. 152), grated Cheddar and shredded lettuce.

Tips

- Nicely balanced with carbohydrate, protein and fats
- Good option for a post-exercise recovery meal
- High in protein, fibre and vitamin C
- Serve with rice to increase the carbs

Eileen's Roast Pork Tenderloin with Honey Apples

SERVES	PREP TIME	COOKING TIME	CALORIES per serving (391g)	CARBS (g)	PROTEIN (g)	FAT (g)	FIBRE (g)
3	10 mins	30 mins	503	21	46	26	3.4

 Rest Day Recipe

Don't knock this recipe till you've tried it – the sweet honey apples and pork combine to create an incredible flavour. This is one I robbed from my mammy, Eileen. I would come home at the weekend from college, Eileen would put this amazing dish in front of me and I'd wolf it down in minutes.

INGREDIENTS

1 large pork fillet, fat cut away
2 tbsp olive oil
1 tbsp soy sauce
1 medium onion, peeled and chopped
2 cloves of garlic, peeled and crushed
sea salt and freshly ground black pepper
1 red pepper, deseeded and chopped
1 cooking apple, chopped into chunks
1 tbsp honey
2 tbsp fresh rosemary, chopped

PREPARATION

1. Preheat oven to 190°C. Butter a medium-sized casserole dish that has a lid.
2. Chop the pork into medallions, roughly bite size. (If you prefer, you can cook the fillet whole and chop when cooked; either method works.)
3. Heat the oil in a large, non-stick pan and sauté the pork over a medium to high heat with the soy sauce, onion, garlic, salt and pepper till lightly brown on both sides, then add the chopped red pepper and cook for 10 minutes.
4. In a bowl, mix the chunks of apple with the honey until nicely coated.
5. Transfer the pork and vegetables from the pan to your dish and stir in the honey apples.
6. Put the lid on the dish and transfer to the oven for 20 minutes, spooning the juices over the pork after 10 minutes to add flavour and moisture to the meat.
7. Garnish with fresh rosemary and serve with roast vegetables and mashed potato.

Tips

- Good for muscle gainers to consume on a workout day
- When served with rice or potato, it becomes an excellent recovery meal

A high-protein, low-carbohydrate meal

Epic Chicken Tikka with Basmati Rice

SERVES	PREP TIME	COOKING TIME	CALORIES per serving (673g)	CARBS (g)	PROTEIN (g)	FAT (g)	FIBRE (g)
3	10 mins	35 mins	643	34	63	28	6

 Rest Day Recipe

This chicken tikka is not the quickest recipe, but if you like authentic Indian flavours it's right up there. This is a high-protein and relatively high-calorie meal due to the cream, olive oil and Greek yoghurt. However, with rice you get a good combination of carbs, fats and protein, which makes it a good recovery meal after a tough training session or workout.

INGREDIENTS

1 tbsp olive oil
1 large onion, peeled and chopped
2 cloves of garlic, peeled and crushed
a thumb-sized piece of fresh ginger, peeled and grated or finely chopped
4 free range chicken breasts, chopped
½ tsp ground cumin
½ tsp paprika
½ tsp ground turmeric
½ tsp garam masala
½ tsp ground coriander
1 tbsp chicken tikka paste (if not using the 5 spices above)
2 red peppers, deseeded and chopped small
1 tbsp mango chutney
1½ 400g tins chopped tomatoes
150 ml cream
2 tbsp Greek yoghurt
100g white or brown Basmati rice

PREPARATION

1. Heat the oil in a large non-stick pan on a medium heat. Add the onion, garlic and ginger and cook for 2 to 3 minutes.
2. Once the onions start to turn brown, add the chicken.
3. Cook the chicken for 4 to 5 minutes then add in the tikka spices (cumin through coriander) or the chicken tikka paste.
4. Next add the peppers, mix and cook for 2 to 3 minutes.
5. Add the mango chutney and stir well.
6. Pour in the chopped tomatoes and stir well, then allow to simmer gently for about 15 minutes.
7. Meanwhile get the rice going. Bring 300ml of water to a boil in a medium-sized saucepan, add the rice, stir, and reduce to a simmer. Cook the rice until the water is almost gone and the rice is soft but not mushy, about 10 to 12 minutes. Leave to rest while you finish the curry.
8. By now the tikka sauce should be starting to reduce down. Stir in the cream, followed by the yoghurt. Serve piping hot in bowls, spooned over the rice.

Tips

- Ultra-satisfying if you've worked up an appetite
- Perfect rest day meal due to the combination of slow-digesting carbohydrates and proteins

The Goliath Burger Bowl

SERVES	PREP TIME	COOKING TIME	CALORIES per serving (860g)	CARBS (g)	PROTEIN (g)	FAT (g)	FIBRE (g)
2	10 mins	25 mins	599	30	50	32	11

 Rest Day Recipe

For a healthier take on the traditional burger, try the Goliath burger bowl, a burger fit for a giant's appetite. With a big serving of protein, the Goliath burger bowl would be suitable for your recovery-focused days. As an added bonus, this meal is high in vitamin C, which is good for your immune function.

INGREDIENTS

1 red pepper, deseeded and chopped
1 yellow pepper, deseeded and chopped
6 mushrooms, chopped
1 tsp sea salt
¼ tsp dried oregano
¼ tsp smoked paprika
¼ tsp ground cumin
¼ tsp garlic powder
300g minced beef steak
2 tbsp olive oil
1 free range egg, beaten
1 tbsp tomato purée
1 medium onion, peeled and chopped
1 tbsp Worcester sauce
50g Cheddar cheese, grated
a handful of baby spinach leaves, washed
a squeeze of lemon juice
6 piccolo tomatoes
½ an avocado, flesh sliced
freshly ground black pepper

PREPARATION

1. Preheat your oven to 180°C.
2. Toss the peppers and mushrooms in a bowl with ½ tsp salt, the oregano, smoked paprika, cumin, garlic powder and 1 tbsp of olive oil.
3. Spread out the vegetables on a baking tray lined with greaseproof paper and roast in the oven for 15 to 20 minutes.
4. Mix the beef with ½ tsp salt, olive oil, the egg, tomato purée, chopped onion and Worcester sauce.
5. Using clean hands, form the mixture into 1 large burger or 2 smaller burgers.
6. Preheat a non-stick pan, add the burger/s and fry for 2 minutes each side to seal and brown a little.
7. Transfer to a baking dish and place in the oven with the spiced veg for 15 minutes or until the burger is cooked to your liking.
8. Remove from the oven, sprinkle the grated cheese over the burgers, then return to the oven for a minute to allow the cheese to melt.
9. Put the spinach leaves in a large bowl and squeeze some lemon juice over.
10. Next take out your burger and put it in the centre of the bowl on the spinach leaves.
11. Remove the peppers and mushrooms from the oven and arrange them around the edges of the burger.
12. Lastly, put the tomatoes and avocado on top of the burger, grind over some black pepper and devour!

Roast Stuffed Peppers with Chicken

SERVES	PREP TIME	COOKING TIME	CALORIES per serving (720g)	CARBS (g)	PROTEIN (g)	FAT (g)	FIBRE (g)
2	10 mins	25 mins	500	31	48	20	12

 Rest Day Recipe

This is a fantastic recipe for anyone who wants to eat a high-protein low-calorie meal. It is tasty and satisfying, which is exactly what you want when eating lower-calorie meals. This meal is also low in carbohydrate, making it a great meal if it's one of those days when you haven't done much physical activity or exercise.

INGREDIENTS

4 peppers of different colours, halved and deseeded
2 tbsp olive oil
1 onion, peeled and chopped
10 mushrooms, halved
2 cloves of garlic, peeled
2 free range chicken breasts, chopped into small pieces
½ tsp smoked paprika
½ tsp chilli powder
½ tsp dried oregano
a handful of spinach leaves, washed
1 400g tin of chopped tomatoes
2 tbsp tomato purée
a handful of fresh spinach, washed
2 tbsp Cheddar cheese, grated

PREPARATION

1. Preheat the oven to 190°C.
2. Place the halved peppers hollow side up on a baking tray, drizzle over 1 tbsp of olive oil and sprinkle on some salt. Cover with foil and bake in the oven for 15 minutes, until soft.
3. To make the chicken and veg filling, warm 1 tbsp of olive oil in a non-stick frying pan over a medium heat. Add the onion, mushrooms and garlic and fry for 3 minutes, then add the chicken, season with the paprika, chilli and oregano and cook for 5 minutes.
4. Add in the chopped tomatoes and tomato purée and cook for 1 or 2 minutes more. Stir in the spinach and cook until it has wilted down.
5. Remove the peppers from the oven and carefully spoon in the chicken filling. Sprinkle the cheese on top and return to the oven for another 5 minutes, until the chicken is completely cooked through and the cheese has melted.

Tips

- Low calorie, low carb and high in protein
- Great source of fibre
- Nutritional bonus – excellent source of vitamin C

One-Pot Meatballs

SERVES	PREP TIME	COOKING TIME	CALORIES per serving (553g)	CARBS (g)	PROTEIN (g)	FAT (g)	FIBRE (g)
3	10 mins	25 mins	534	16	50	30	5.5

 Rest Day Recipe

These one-pot meatballs can be whipped up in 25 minutes and served as a delicious high-protein evening meal. Eat with rice or potato to add some carbohydrate for energy on your training days or simply on their own with some vegetables if you don't need the extra carbs.

INGREDIENTS

For the sauce:
1 tbsp olive oil
1 white onion, peeled and diced
2 cloves of garlic, peeled and finely chopped
½ a red chilli, deseeded and finely chopped
½ tsp ground cumin
1 tsp paprika
200g cherry tomatoes, halved

1 400 g tin of chopped tomatoes

For the meatballs:
500g lean minced beef
2 eggs, beaten
2 tbsp extra virgin olive oil
½ a red onion, finely chopped
1 tsp ground cumin
2 large garlic cloves, peeled and crushed
½ tsp paprika

1 tbsp tomato purée
zest of ½ a lime
½ tsp dried mixed herbs
sea salt and freshly ground black pepper

To finish:
1 small head of broccoli, broken into florets
50g grated Cheddar cheese

PREPARATION

1. Preheat oven to 180°C.
2. For the sauce, get a non-stick, oven-friendly frying pan, heat the olive oil and sauté the onion for 2 minutes over a medium heat until beginning to soften.
3. Add the garlic, chilli, cumin and paprika and continue to cook on a low heat for 1 minute. Add the cherry tomatoes followed by the tinned tomatoes and mix together. Simmer on a low heat while you make the meatballs.
4. Combine all the meatball ingredients in a bowl and mix well so everything is combined and bound together. Using clean hands, roll the mixture into balls of desired size – roughly 1 tbsp works well. Place them on a plate as you make them. When you have all the meatballs made, add them to a clean non-stick frying pan with a little oil, one by one. Cook on a high heat for 1 to 2 minutes, turning regularly until browned.
5. Tip the browned meatballs into the pan of tomato sauce, mix together, then dot the broccoli florets between them. Scatter the Cheddar cheese on top and place in the oven for 10 minutes until bubbling.

Roast Peppers with Lentils and Quinoa

SERVES	PREP TIME	COOKING TIME	CALORIES per serving (703g)	CARBS (g)	PROTEIN (g)	FAT (g)	FIBRE (g)
3	10 mins	20 mins	622	56	30	32	17

 Exercise Day Recipe

This is a fantastic recipe for anyone who wants to eat a high-protein plant-based meal. It is tasty and nutritious while meeting all targets for energy and key nutrients like essential fats and amino acids. If you are highly active or aiming to hit your protein needs with grains and lentils this is a super option.

INGREDIENTS

130g red lentils
150g quinoa
6 peppers of various colours, deseeded and halved
2 tbsp olive oil
1 onion, peeled and diced
2 cloves of garlic, peeled and chopped
a pinch of sea salt
1 courgette, diced
1 400g tin of chopped tomatoes
2 tbsp Cheddar cheese, grated

For the hummus:

1 400g tin of chickpeas, drained
1 tbsp tahini
1 tbsp of olive oil
1 clove of garlic, peeled
1 scallion, chopped
1 tbsp lemon juice
1 tsp ground coriander
½ tsp ground cumin
sea salt and freshly ground pepper to taste

PREPARATION

1. Preheat your oven to 190°C.
2. Place the lentils and quinoa in approximately 400ml water, bring to the boil and simmer for 15 minutes or until almost all the water has evaporated.
3. Place the pepper halves on a baking dish, hollow sides up, sprinkle with a little salt, drizzle over 1 tbsp of olive oil then set aside.
4. In a non-stick pan on a medium heat, cook the onion and garlic with 1 tbsp of olive oil and a pinch of salt. When the onions start to turn brown add the finely chopped courgette and stir. Cook until the courgette is starting to brown.
5. Add the tinned tomatoes, stir well, then stir through the cooked quinoa and lentils (making sure there is no water left in the lentils and quinoa). Cook for 4 to 5 minutes until the moisture has reduced. Taste to see if you want to add salt and pepper.
6. Fill the 8 pepper halves with the quinoa and lentil mixture then place them in the oven.
7. Bake for about 10 minutes then remove, sprinkle the cheese on top and put back the oven for another 5 to 10 minutes or until the edge of the peppers start to turn brown.
8. To make the hummus, blend the chickpeas, tahini, olive oil, garlic, scallion, lemon juice, coriander, cumin and salt and pepper until smooth.
9. Remove the stuffed peppers from the oven and serve topped with the hummus.

Spicy Beef Burgers with Homemade Relish

SERVES	PREP TIME	COOKING TIME	CALORIES per serving (729g)	CARBS (g)	PROTEIN (g)	FAT (g)	FIBRE (g)
2	30 mins	30 mins	544	25	58	20	4

 Rest Day Recipe

Nothing beats making your own beef burgers! You know exactly what's in them and you can make them taste how you like with fresh spices and herbs. This beef burger recipe provides a massive 58g of protein. As the burgers need to be refrigerated before cooking, you'll need to start making them a while before you want to eat them!

INGREDIENTS

1 free range egg
1 clove of garlic, peeled and crushed
½ tsp. dried basil
½ tsp. chilli powder
a pinch of sea salt and freshly ground black pepper
500g lean beef mince
1 red onion, peeled and finely chopped
1 tbsp olive oil

For the relish:

1 red chilli, deseeded and finely chopped
1 onion, peeled and sliced
1 clove of garlic, peeled and crushed
1 tbsp olive oil
1 tsp sea salt
1 400g tin of chopped tomatoes
1 tbsp honey
100ml white wine vinegar
a handful of fresh coriander
1 tsp mild curry powder

PREPARATION

1. In a small bowl, beat the egg with the garlic, basil, chilli, salt and pepper.
2. Place the beef mince in a large bowl, and mix through the chopped onion with clean hands.
3. Next, add the egg mix to the beef and mix again using your hands until everything is well bound together. Form into 4 burgers, put on a plate and refrigerate for 30 minutes, to firm up.
4. Preheat the oven to 190°C.
5. Remove the burgers from the fridge, place on a baking tray greased with olive oil and cook for 20 to 30 minutes depending on how well you like your burgers done. Note: If you are in a hurry you can grill or pan-fry the burgers for 3 to 6 minutes each side.
6. For the relish, first fry the onion, garlic and chilli in a pan with the olive oil and salt over a medium heat. Then add in the tomatoes and honey and stir.
7. Add the vinegar, coriander and curry powder and simmer for 30 minutes until it has reduced down to a thick relish consistency.
8. Serve the burgers with the relish and any other toppings you fancy!

 Tips

- **Provides a mega hit of protein and is very low in carbohydrates**

Spicy Cod with Plum Tomatoes

SERVES	PREP TIME	COOKING TIME	CALORIES per serving (536g)	CARBS (g)	PROTEIN (g)	FAT (g)	FIBRE (g)
3	5 mins	20 mins	261	14	30	9.9	5.4

 Rest Day Recipe

Chilli and cod get on like a house on fire in this quick and tasty recipe. Spicy cod is one of our lightest meals on the menu – it's easily digestible, low in calories and a great source of protein.

INGREDIENTS

2 tbsp olive oil
1 medium onion, peeled and chopped
1 garlic clove, peeled and chopped
1 red chilli, diced
sea salt and freshly ground black pepper
1 400g tin of plum tomatoes
½ a stick of celery, chopped
10 piccolo tomatoes, chopped
a handful of spinach, washed
1 red pepper, deseeded and chopped
1 yellow pepper, deseeded and chopped
4 pieces of fresh cod, approximately 500g
a few sprigs of fresh dill, chopped
a few sprigs of fresh oregano, leaves chopped
juice of 1 lemon
a drizzle of olive oil, to serve

PREPARATION

1. Heat the oil in a large pan over a medium heat. Add the onion, chillies and garlic and sauté for 5 minutes, then season with salt and pepper.
2. Add the tinned tomatoes, celery, fresh piccolo tomatoes, spinach and a little water and cook for 2 to 3 minutes, stirring regularly.
3. Add in the chopped peppers, stir well and cook for another 10 minutes.
4. Pat the fish fillets dry with a kitchen towel then season with salt and pepper. Place carefully into the tomato and spinach mixture. Cover the pan and cook on a gentle heat for 12 to 15 minutes, until flesh is opaque.
5. Before removing from heat, scatter the herbs, then stir in the lemon juice. Finish with a drizzle of olive oil on top.

Tips

- A light meal that is equally light in calories
- High in protein
- Cook with some chorizo to make a delicious Spanish-style dish

Spicy Mince Bonanza

SERVES	PREP TIME	COOKING TIME	CALORIES per serving (823g)	CARBS (g)	PROTEIN (g)	FAT (g)	FIBRE (g)
3	10 mins	30 mins	646	68	46	17	14

 *Exercise Day Recipe*

This recipe combines potatoes, vegetables and a spicy mince to create an excellent recovery meal. The combination of carbohydrate from the potato and protein from the minced beef will provide the optimum nutrients to replenish your body after an exercise session.

INGREDIENTS

1 potato, cut into chip shapes
2 sweet potatoes, cut into chip shapes
1 parsnip, peeled and cut into chip shapes
1/3 of a butternut squash, peeled and cut into chip shapes
a pinch of sea salt
1 tsp paprika
1 tsp ground cumin
2 tbsp olive oil
1 large onion, peeled and chopped
1 clove of garlic, peeled and chopped
500g minced beef
1 red pepper, deseeded and chopped
8 mushrooms, chopped
½ a courgette, chopped
1 400g tin of chopped tomatoes
2 tbsp tomato purée
½ tsp chilli flakes
½ tsp dried oregano
2 tbsp strong Cheddar, grated

PREPARATION

1. Preheat the oven to 200°C.
2. Toss the chopped chip-shaped veg with salt, paprika and cumin, then spread them out on a baking dish lined with baking paper. Put in the hot oven for 30 minutes, stirring everything around after 15 minutes to ensure all the veg cook evenly.
3. Put the olive oil in a large non-stick pan over a medium heat. Add the onion and garlic, cook for 2 to 3 minutes, then add in the minced beef and cook until most of it turns brown, stirring regularly to cook the meat evenly.
4. Add in the pepper, mushrooms and courgette and cook, mixing regularly, for 4 to 5 minutes.
5. Next add in the chopped tomatoes and tomato purée and mix again, adding chilli flakes, oregano and a pinch of salt.
6. Remove the chopped vegetables from the oven, which should now be turning crispy, and mix well to prevent them sticking together. Pour over the spicy beef and sprinkle the grated Cheddar over everything. Put back in the oven for 2 minutes until the cheese is melted and bubbling nicely.

Sweet Chilli Steak Fajita Bowl

SERVES	PREP TIME	COOKING TIME	CALORIES per serving (1000g)	CARBS (g)	PROTEIN (g)	FAT (g)	FIBRE (g)
1	5 mins	20 mins	941	63	77	42	19

 Exercise Day Recipe

This is a monster of a meal, so you need to have exercised intensely to deserve it! If you're not feeling the appetite of a beast, split into two portions for half the calories and macros.

INGREDIENTS

1½ tsp chilli powder
1 tsp ground cumin
1 tsp garlic powder
1 tsp onion powder
½ tsp smoked paprika
¼ teaspoon sea salt
2 tbsp olive oil
juice of 1 lime
1 tbsp soy sauce
300g lean beef steak, cut into slices
100g white rice
1 onion, peeled and sliced into wedges
2 cloves of garlic, peeled and chopped
1 red pepper, deseeded and sliced into strips
1 yellow pepper, deseeded and sliced into strips

For the toppings:
⅛ teaspoon black pepper or to taste
avocado slices or guacamole
fresh coriander
lime wedges
2 tbsp yoghurt mixed with 1 tbsp sweet chilli sauce

PREPARATION

1. In a small bowl, combine the chilli powder, cumin, garlic powder, onion powder, paprika, salt and pepper. Reserve 1½ teaspoons for the vegetables.
2. In a bowl, combine 1 tbsp olive oil, lime juice, soy sauce and spices. Add the steak slices and combine everything thoroughly to flavour the meat.
3. When the steak is marinating, put the rice in a small saucepan with 250ml boiling water and simmer until cooked, roughly 10 to 12 minutes.
4. Heat 1 tbsp of olive oil in a non-stick pan over medium-high heat. Add the onion and garlic and cook for 4 to 5 minutes, shaking the pan regularly. Add the peppers and sprinkle with the reserved fajita spices. If you like the peppers with a nice crunch, cook for about 3 minutes; if you like them softer, leave them on for about 2 to 3 minutes longer. Transfer and set aside on a plate.
5. Wipe out the same pan with some kitchen paper then sear the steak in 1 tbsp of olive oil. Allow to cook for 3 to 4 minutes (depending how well cooked you like it) on each side.
6. Now it's time to assemble your fajita bowl! Fill 1 or 2 bowls with rice and top with steak, onions and peppers. Finish off with your choice of toppings.

Steak with Sweet Potato and Parsnip Chips

SERVES	PREP TIME	COOKING TIME	CALORIES per serving (995g)	CARBS (g)	PROTEIN (g)	FAT (g)	FIBRE (g)
1	5 mins	20–30 mins	694	80	44	22	18

 Exercise Day Recipe

This is a straightforward recipe that is still super-tasty and satisfying. Sweet potato is the main carbohydrate source, but the parsnip chips also provide a decent source of carbohydrate. Together they enable a sustained release of energy to your body.

INGREDIENTS

1 steak of choice – sirloin, ribeye or fillet

2 parsnips, peeled and cut into thin strips

2 sweet potatoes, cut into thin strips

olive oil

a pinch of ground cumin

a pinch of sea salt

2 cloves of garlic, peeled and crushed

a few springs of fresh thyme, leaves picked

PREPARATION

1. Remove the steak from the fridge, unwrap from its packaging and allow it to come to room temperature, about 20 minutes.
2. Preheat your oven to 200°C.
3. In a bowl toss the parsnip and sweet potato pieces together with some olive oil, cumin and salt.
4. Spread in a single layer on a baking tray and bake for 15 to 30 minutes (depending on the size of the strips) or until golden brown, flipping halfway through.
5. Meanwhile, prepare your steak. Brush each side with a little olive oil, rub in the fresh garlic and season with some salt.
6. Put the steak in a hot non-stick oven-proof griddle pan and cook for about 2 minutes on each side. Transfer to the oven for 4 to 5 minutes.
7. When the steak is cooked to your liking, remove from the oven, put on a warmed plate and allow to rest for about 4 minutes.
8. Remove your veg chips from the oven and sprinkle generously with the thyme leaves, and extra salt and pepper to taste. Serve with the steak.

Can support carb-loading prior to an event or performance

Tips

- High-protein and carbohydrate meal that's ideal for pre- or post-exercise performance
- Excellent source of protein, 78 per cent of which comes from steak

Sweet Potato and Carrot Fish Pie

SERVES	PREP TIME	COOKING TIME	CALORIES per serving (850g)	CARBS (g)	PROTEIN (g)	FAT (g)	FIBRE (g)
3	10 mins	40 mins	726	92	34	25	16

 Exercise Day Recipe

This one's a fish pie with a twist as the sweet potato and carrots offer a flavoursome alternative to the typical mashed potato topping. You can of course vary the fish and the veg to your taste. The quality protein and omega-3 fatty acids in this meal make it an ideal as a recovery meal.

INGREDIENTS

2 large sweet potatoes, peeled and chopped
2 carrots, peeled and chopped
1 tsp sea salt
½ tsp freshly ground black pepper
a knob of butter
400g fish pie mix (e.g. smoked haddock, cod, salmon)
150g prawns
200ml cream
1 garlic clove, peeled and finely chopped
1 red onion, peeled and chopped
1 head of broccoli, florets chopped
a handful of spinach, washed
1 courgette, chopped
2 tbsp strong Cheddar cheese, grated

PREPARATION

1. Preheat the oven to 190°C.
2. Steam the sweet potato and carrots until soft then mash with a little salt, pepper and butter and set aside while you prepare your fish.
3. Mix the fish and prawns together in a bowl with the cream, garlic and chopped vegetables.
4. Transfer to a large pot and cook the mixture for 10 minutes before tipping carefully into a baking dish.
5. Spread the sweet potato and carrot mash over the top of the mixture and bake in the oven for 20 minutes. Remove the dish from the oven, scatter the grated cheese on top, then return for another 10 minutes until the top is golden and the cheese is melted.

Tips

- **Great option for a post-workout recovery meal**
- **Fish provides a good source of omega-3 fatty acids**
- **Use less cream if you want to reduce the calories**

Sweet Potato Lasagne

SERVES	PREP TIME	COOKING TIME	CALORIES per serving (682g)	CARBS (g)	PROTEIN (g)	FAT (g)	FIBRE (g)
5	10 mins	40 mins	690	45	60	31	6.6

 Exercise Day Recipe

Sweet potato slices replace the pasta in this spin on traditional lasagne. It's a dream combination of slow-digesting and nutritious sweet potato and high-protein beef. You will not believe the speed it disappears when you place it in front of your family or friends!

INGREDIENTS

3 large sweet potatoes, cut lengthways into long, thin slices
500g cottage cheese
1 egg
500g Greek yoghurt
2 tbsp olive oil
1 tbsp fresh parsley, chopped
600g lean beef mince
50g chorizo, diced
3 cloves of garlic, peeled and chopped
1 onion, peeled and diced
1 tbsp dried oregano
½ tsp salt
1 tsp ground cumin
8 mushrooms, sliced
1 400g tin of chopped tomatoes
2 tbsp tomato purée
¼ tsp freshly ground black pepper
100g mozzarella, sliced
50g aged red Cheddar, grated

PREPARATION

1. Steam the sweet potato slices until tender but not soft, about 15 minutes. Set aside.
2. Now make the sauce. In a medium bowl, combine the cottage cheese with the egg, yoghurt, 1 tbsp of olive oil and parsley. Mix well and then set aside.
3. Heat 1 tbsp of olive oil over medium-high heat in a large pan. Add the beef, chorizo, garlic, onion, oregano, salt and cumin. Cook this mixture, stirring regularly, until it becomes well browned, roughly 5 minutes.
4. Add in the mushrooms and cook for an additional 4 to 5 minutes. Add the tomatoes and tomato purée into the pan and stir to mix well. Simmer for another few minutes, seasoning with a few grinds of black pepper.
5. Now it's time to assemble your lasagne. Butter a medium-sized casserole dish and arrange the first layer with half of the sweet potato slices, making them overlap.
6. Pour half the meat sauce over the sweet potato slices and spread out evenly. Pour half of the cottage cheese mixture over the meat sauce and spread evenly.
7. Repeat the process with another layer of sweet potato slices, meat sauce and then the cottage cheese sauce.
8. Top with a thin layer of fresh mozzarella and grated red Cheddar and then cover with tin foil.
9. Place in the oven and bake for 30 minutes, taking the foil cover off for the last 5 minutes to allow the top to brown.

Sweet Potato Seafood Chowder

SERVES	PREP TIME	COOKING TIME	CALORIES per serving (727g)	CARBS (g)	PROTEIN (g)	FAT (g)	FIBRE (g)
3	10 mins	35 mins	632	50	50	26	8.6

 Exercise Day Recipe

One for all the seafood lovers out there! Mix and match your seafood preference for an enjoyable and easily digestible chowder. Fish provides a good source of both protein and fat with many healthy omega-3 fatty acids. I recommend having this chowder following exercise as the quality sources of sweet potato and protein are great for your recovery.

INGREDIENTS

500ml whole milk
500g cod, salmon and
   smoked haddock mix
80g king prawns
1 tbsp olive oil
1 large onion, peeled and
   chopped
2 garlic cloves, peeled and
   chopped
2 medium-sized sweet
   potatoes/regular potatoes,
   peeled and chopped
1 head of broccoli, chopped
   into florets
3 large carrots, chopped
200ml cream
sea salt and freshly ground
   black pepper
1 tbsp fresh parsley,
   chopped

PREPARATION

1. Poach the fish mix and prawns in the milk in a large pot over a medium heat for 10 minutes.
2. When cooked, tip the fish and milk mixture into a large bowl and set aside.
3. Heat the oil in a large pan over a medium heat. Add the onion and garlic and fry for 5 minutes.
4. Add the sweet potatoes, broccoli and carrots, and sauté for 5 minutes.
5. Carefully strain the milk from the fish into a wide jug and put the fish on a plate. Pour the milk into the vegetable mix, then stir in the cream.
6. Simmer for 25 minutes on a medium heat until the sweet potatoes/potatoes are soft. Return the fish to the pan, stir through gently and season with salt and pepper. Serve, piping hot, in bowls, with some parsley scattered over the top.

Tips

- **Great option for a post-workout recovery meal**
- **Fish provides a good source of omega-3 fatty acids**

Sweet Potato Thai Red Curry

SERVES	PREP TIME	COOKING TIME	CALORIES per serving (623g)	CARBS (g)	PROTEIN (g)	FAT (g)	FIBRE (g)
3	10 mins	30 mins	820	56	43	48	11

 Exercise Day Recipe

This is one of those standout meals that you genuinely look forward to having in the evening. There is an excellent combination of slow-digesting carbohydrate from the sweet potato, and the chicken provides three-quarters of the protein.

INGREDIENTS

2–3 free range chicken breasts
sea salt and freshly ground black pepper
1½ tbsp olive oil
1 small onion, peeled and finely diced
2 cloves of garlic, peeled and crushed
2 red chillis, deseeded and finely chopped
a thumb-sized piece of fresh ginger, peeled and finely diced
2 tbsp good-quality Thai red curry paste
1 400 ml tin of coconut milk
2 sweet potatoes, peeled and chopped
2 carrots, chopped
1 red pepper, deseeded and chopped
juice of 1 lime
1 tsp honey
a handful of fresh coriander
a handful of fresh basil
3 tbsp cashew nuts
natural yoghurt

PREPARATION

1. Preheat the oven to 180°C.
2. Season the chicken with salt and pepper, place on a baking tray lined with greaseproof paper, drizzle over ½ tbsp olive oil and bake in the oven for 15 minutes.
3. In a saucepan on a medium-high heat, heat 1 tbsp of olive oil then add the onion, garlic, chillies and ginger. Stir continuously for a couple of minutes, being careful not to let it burn.
4. Mix through the red curry paste and cook for 3 minutes.
5. Next pour in the coconut milk and bring to a gentle simmer for 5 minutes.
6. Add the chopped sweet potato, carrots, pepper, lime juice and honey, and continue to simmer.
7. Remove the chicken from oven, chop into bite-sized pieces and add to the curry.
8. Once the sweet potato is cooked through, the curry is ready (about 15 minutes).
9. Add chopped coriander and basil, and finish with some toasted cashew nuts.
10. Serve on its own with a dollop of natural yoghurt, adding a portion of rice if you want added carbohydrate.

 Tips

- **Provides twice your daily requirement of vitamin A**

Teriyaki Salmon with Chilli-Roast Vegetables

SERVES	PREP TIME	COOKING TIME	CALORIES per serving (540g)	CARBS (g)	PROTEIN (g)	FAT (g)	FIBRE (g)
3	10 mins	30 mins	432	53	24	14	12

 Exercise Day Recipe

Did you know ... teriyaki is a mixture of soy sauce, sake and ginger, used in Japanese cookery as a marinade for fish or meat dishes? It features in this tasty, sticky, filling and easy-to-make meal, an ideal dinner option that contains lots of fibre, protein and healthy fats.

INGREDIENTS

1 sweet potato, peeled and chopped

1 parsnip, peeled and chopped

2 red peppers, deseeded and chopped

2 carrots, chopped

1 red onion, peeled and cut into wedges

a head of broccoli, florets roughly chopped

2 tbsp olive oil

1 tsp chilli flakes

1 tsp paprika

pinch of sea salt

½ a thumb-sized piece of fresh ginger, peeled and finely chopped

1 garlic clove, peeled and finely chopped

1 small red chilli, deseeded and chopped

zest and juice of 1 lime

2 tbsp honey

5 tbsp dark soy sauce

2 large salmon fillets

a bunch of fresh coriander, chopped

PREPARATION

1. Preheat the oven to 180°C.
2. Spread the sweet potato, parsnip, peppers, carrots, red onion and broccoli on a baking tray lined with greaseproof paper. Drizzle with 1 tbsp of olive oil, season with chilli flakes and paprika, and roast in the oven for 30 minutes.
3. While the vegetables roast, heat 1 tbsp of olive oil in a pan on medium-high heat, and fry the ginger, garlic and chilli with a pinch of salt for 3 minutes.
4. Add the lime zest and juice, honey and soy sauce, and cook until reduced and sticky.
5. Meanwhile pat the salmon fillets dry with kitchen paper then sear in a hot griddle pan for 2 minutes on each side.
6. When the sauce is reduced, place the salmon in a baking dish and pour the teriyaki sauce on top.
7. Bake in the oven for 15 minutes until the salmon is cooked through. Sprinkle the fresh coriander on top and serve.

Tips

- **Contains healthy fats and protein from the salmon**
- **Great recovery meal option**

Sweet Potato Shepherd's Pie

SERVES	PREP TIME	COOKING TIME	CALORIES per serving (688g)	CARBS (g)	PROTEIN (g)	FAT (g)	FIBRE (g)
4	10 mins	40 mins	586	85	34	13	13

 Exercise Day Recipe

A simple recipe like this comforting shepherd's pie is an ideal refuel and recovery meal after training. The sweet potato provides carbohydrate, the beef supplies a quality source of protein and the mix of vegetables delivers an array of essential micronutrients.

INGREDIENTS

3 large sweet potatoes, peeled and chopped
1 tbsp olive oil
1 onion, peeled and chopped
1 clove of garlic, peeled and chopped
2 tsp cumin
1 tsp chilli flakes
400g lean minced beef
1 red bell pepper, deseeded and finely chopped
1 yellow bell pepper, deseeded and finely chopped
8 mushrooms, chopped
3 tbsp tomato purée
50g frozen peas
30g sugar snap peas
¼ tsp ground cinnamon
¼ tsp ground nutmeg
2 tsp Worcester sauce
a knob of butter
sea salt and freshly ground black pepper
50g strong Cheddar cheese, grated

PREPARATION

1. Preheat the oven to 190°C.
2. Steam the sweet potatoes for 20 minutes until tender, and set aside.
3. Put the oil in a large non-stick pan on a medium heat. Add the onion, garlic, cumin and chilli flakes and cook until starting to brown. Add the beef and stir continuously until this also starts to brown, about 5 minutes.
4. Reduce the heat to low. Stir in the peppers, mushrooms, tomato purée, peas, sugar snap peas, cinnamon, nutmeg and Worcester sauce. Cover and simmer for 10 minutes.
5. Meanwhile, prepare your topping. Mash the cooked sweet potatoes in a bowl with the butter, salt and pepper.
6. Pour the beef and vegetable mixture into a medium-sized baking dish.
7. Spread the mashed sweet potato over the beef and sprinkle the Cheddar cheese on top.
8. Put in the oven and bake for 15 to 20 minutes until the top is golden brown and the cheese is bubbling.

Tips

- **Fuel-up or recovery recipe**
- **Great for filling fibre**

No-Fuss Chickpea and Edamame Pilaf

SERVES	PREP TIME	COOKING TIME	CALORIES per serving (570g)	CARBS (g)	PROTEIN (g)	FAT (g)	FIBRE (g)
4	10 mins	15 mins	480	57	22.2	15	10.5

 Exercise Day Recipe

Rice, chickpeas, edamame and carrots combine in this recipe to provide a tasty meat-free protein-rich dish. The harissa and stock combine to create a lovely combination of flavours. It contains a good proportion of carbs and a moderate amount of protein making it an ideal option both before and after exercise.

INGREDIENTS

1 tbsp olive oil
2 onions, peeled and finely chopped
3 carrots, coarsely grated
2 tbsp harissa paste
300g basmati rice, rinsed
700ml vegetable stock, made with 1 stock cube
1 400g tin of chickpeas, drained
150g cooked edamame beans (available frozen in Asian supermarkets)
25g flaked almonds, toasted in a dry frying pan
200g Greek yoghurt

PREPARATION

1. Heat the oil in a lidded casserole dish, add the onions and cook until soft.
2. Tip in the grated carrots, harissa and rice, and stir for a couple of minutes.
3. Pour in the hot stock, bring to the boil, then cover with the lid and simmer gently for 10 minutes.
4. Mix in the chickpeas and edamame beans and cook gently for 5 minutes more, until the grains of rice are tender and all the liquid has been absorbed.
5. Turn off the heat, cover and leave to sit for a few minutes.
6. Serve in bowls with a sprinkle of almonds and a dollop of yoghurt on each serving.

Tips

- High-carbohydrate meal to fuel the body for exercise
- Super plant-based protein meal
- Excellent recovery meal option

Excellent vegetarian option

Spicy Green Coconut Curry

SERVES	PREP TIME	COOKING TIME	CALORIES per serving (405g)	CARBS (g)	PROTEIN (g)	FAT (g)	FIBRE (g)
2	10 mins	20 mins	573	14	37	40	6.4

 Rest Day Recipe

This curry makes for a brilliant, filling evening meal. The spice provided by the chillies combines really well with the sweetness of the coconut milk to create a mild-tasting curry sauce for those averse to too much spice. Perfect for that 'takeaway' vibe on a Friday or Saturday night.

INGREDIENTS

1 tbsp coconut oil
1 clove of garlic, peeled and crushed
1 red chilli, deseeded and diced (leave the seeds in if you like it hot)
2 free range chicken breasts, evenly sliced
2 carrots, finely chopped
50g broccoli, chopped
80g green beans, diced
½ tbsp fish sauce
1 tbsp soy sauce
1 400g tin of coconut milk
20g cashew nuts, unsalted
1 tbsp fresh basil
sea salt and freshly ground black pepper

PREPARATION

1. Heat the coconut oil in a wok over a medium heat and add the garlic and chilli.
2. After a minute of gentle sautéing, add the chicken and cook for 5 minutes or until light gold, stirring regularly.
3. Add the carrots, broccoli and beans before stirring in the fish and soy sauce followed by the coconut milk.
4. Allow to simmer for a few minutes, then mix through the cashew nuts and fresh basil. Season with salt and pepper.
5. Serve with white or brown rice.

Tips

- High-protein, low-carbohydrate meal
- Good source of fibre
- For a meat-free alternative, replace chicken with tofu

Hot and Spicy Thai Chicken

SERVES	PREP TIME	COOKING TIME	CALORIES per serving (400g)	CARBS (g)	PROTEIN (g)	FAT (g)	FIBRE (g)
2	10 mins	15 mins	467	13	43	27	6.4

 Rest Day Recipe

This spicy Thai chicken recipe is quick to whip up and combines delicious flavours and textures from the green vegetables, chilli and fresh basil. It's high in protein and nutrients from the chicken and vegetables, and you can enjoy it for either lunch or dinner.

INGREDIENTS

1 tbsp coconut oil
1 clove of garlic, peeled and crushed
1 red chilli, diced (leave seeds in if you like it spicy)
2 free range chicken breasts, evenly sliced
2 carrots, finely chopped
50g broccoli, chopped
80g green beans, diced
½ tbsp fish sauce
1 tbsp soy sauce
½ a 400g tin of coconut milk
sea salt and freshly ground black pepper
10g fresh basil, leaves picked
a squeeze of lime juice

PREPARATION

1. Heat the coconut oil in a wok over a medium heat. Add the garlic and chilli and sauté for a minute.
2. Next add in the chicken and cook for 5 minutes or until light gold, stirring regularly.
3. Add the carrots, broccoli and green beans before stirring in the fish and soy sauce, followed by the coconut milk.
4. Allow to simmer until vegetables are cooked (but retain some 'bite'), then season with salt and pepper. Scatter in the basil leaves and squeeze in the lime juice.
5. Serve with brown or white rice.

 Tips

- **A good option for an evening meal on a rest or recovery day**
- **Low-carbohydrate meal with slow-releasing energy**

Plant Power Buddha Bowl

SERVES	PREP TIME	COOKING TIME	CALORIES per serving (640g)	CARBS (g)	PROTEIN (g)	FAT (g)	FIBRE (g)
2	10 mins	12 mins	720	72	29	31	17

 Exercise Day Recipe

This buddha bowl combines masses of fresh ingredients with eye popping colour. This meal is a real eating experience and the nutrition values are outstanding for a plant-focused meal. You need to marinate the tofu for an hour before you start so you can get ahead with this first.

INGREDIENTS

2 tbsp olive oil

½ tsp sesame oil

1 tsp chilli oil

2 tsp dried thyme

1 tsp paprika

½ tsp salt

200g tofu, drained

1 sweet potato, peeled and diced

1 onion, peeled and sliced

2 cloves of garlic, peeled and minced

1 tbsp peanut or vegetable oil

½ a 400g tin of chickpeas, drained (200 g)

½ tsp sea salt, plus more to taste

½ tsp freshly ground black pepper

1 tsp chilli powder

1 teaspoon garlic powder

250g cooked quinoa (see p. 131 for instructions)

a handful of spinach, washed

1 ripe avocado, sliced

juice of 1 lemon

PREPARATION

1. First make the dressing. In a small bowl, mix the olive, sesame and chilli oils with the thyme, paprika and salt.
2. Place the tofu in the bowl with the dressing and marinate for an hour.
3. Preheat the oven to 200°C.
4. Place the sweet potato, onion and garlic on a baking tray lined with greaseproof paper and toss with the vegetable or peanut oil. Season with salt and pepper, then bake in the oven for 20 to 25 minutes.
5. In a medium bowl, combine the chickpeas, salt, pepper, chilli powder and garlic powder.
6. Transfer the spiced chickpeas to a non-stick pan and cook over medium heat for about 10 minutes.
7. Fry the tofu in the same pan for about 10 minutes on each side.
8. Remove the tofu and cut into cubes.
9. Arrange the quinoa, spinach, roast sweet potatoes and onions, spiced chickpeas and tofu in a medium to large bowl and top off with the sliced avocado and lemon juice.

Tips

- **High-carbohydrate meal to fuel the body for exercise**
- **Super plant-based protein meal**
- **Excellent recovery meal option**

SAVOURY SNACKS

Avocado Toast with Cottage Cheese

SERVES	PREP TIME	COOKING TIME	CALORIES per serving (197g)	CARBS (g)	PROTEIN (g)	FAT (g)	FIBRE (g)
1	3 mins	2 mins	266	29	10	12	6.9

 Exercise Day Recipe

Avocadoes blend really nicely with cottage cheese and tomatoes over a hot slice of toast. This recipe is so easy to put together! Avocado toast and cottage cheese works well for breakfast, pre-exercise or late-night post-workout snack.

INGREDIENTS

2 slices of sourdough brown bread
½ an avocado
2 tbsp cottage cheese
6 piccolo tomatoes, sliced
sea salt and freshly ground black pepper to taste

PREPARATION

1. Toast your bread on a grill or in a toaster.
2. Scoop out the flesh from the avocado, mash with a fork then spoon it on to the slices of toasted bread and spread out evenly.
3. Spread the cottage cheese across the top of the avocado.
4. Lay the sliced tomatoes on top of the cottage cheese, season with salt and pepper and serve.

Tips

- Low in fibre and therefore easily digested
- Great source of potassium from the avocados
- Great post-training snack for muscle recovery due to slow-releasing protein from cottage cheese

Great breakfast or pre-workout option

Chicken Skewers with Guacamole

SERVES	PREP TIME	COOKING TIME	CALORIES per serving (357g)	CARBS (g)	PROTEIN (g)	FAT (g)	FIBRE (g)
3-6	15 mins	15-20 mins	339	13	24	21	7

 Rest Day Recipe

This recipe contains a Mexican-inspired guacamole which is a really tasty way to get heart-friendly, healthy fats into you from avocados. Chicken on a skewer is a fun way of eating – for adults and children alike – and almost has a party feel to it. You'll need some wooden or metal skewers.

INGREDIENTS

For the guacamole:

4 avocados
juice of 1 lime
2 shallots, diced
½ tsp garlic powder
1 small chilli, deseeded
 and finely chopped
¼ tsp sea salt
2 tbsp fresh coriander,
 chopped

For the chicken skewers:

8 tsp mirin
4 tsp soy sauce
1 tsp honey
2–4 free range chicken
 breasts, diced (depending
 on how many people you
 are cooking for)
4 red peppers, evenly
 chopped
2 courgettes, cut into half moons
8 mushrooms, halved
1 red onion, peeled and cut
 into chunks
1 tbsp sesame seeds
3 spring onions, sliced

PREPARATION

1. First prepare your guacamole. Halve each avocado and remove the pit.
2. Scoop the flesh into a bowl, pour in the lime juice and lightly mash the avocado with the shallot, garlic, chilli and salt. Stir through the fresh coriander and set aside.
3. Now prepare your skewers. Mix the mirin, soy sauce and honey in a bowl.
4. Thread chicken, pepper, courgette, mushroom and onion chunks evenly onto your skewers, then brush with the sauce.
5. Heat your grill and cook the skewers for 15 minutes, turning and brushing with the sauce every 5 minutes.
6. When they are cooked, garnish with sesame seeds and spring onions and serve with the guacamole.

Tips

- Great party snack
- Low in carbohydrate with a good protein source from the chicken
- Popular with kids

Mini Skewer Burgers

MAKES	PREP TIME	COOKING TIME	CALORIES per serving (250g)	CARBS (g)	PROTEIN (g)	FAT (g)	FIBRE (g)
8	10 mins	15 mins	270	8.4	34	11	2.3

 Rest Day Recipe

These mini beef burgers work great as a fun protein option for children or even as canapes at parties. Play around with the components of your mini skewers – you can use olives, gherkins, sundried tomatoes or any other vegetables that suit your taste.

INGREDIENTS

500g lean minced beef
1 free range egg
1 onion, peeled and finely chopped
3 cloves of garlic, peeled and crushed
1 tbsp barbecue sauce
1 tbsp tomato purée
1 tsp sea salt
1 tsp freshly ground black pepper
1 tsp olive oil
8 cherry tomatoes, halved
50g Cheddar cheese, cut into cubes
iceberg lettuce, washed and cut into chunks

PREPARATION

1. Preheat the oven to 180°C.
2. In a large bowl, mix together the beef, egg, onion, garlic, barbecue sauce, tomato purée, salt and pepper. With clean hands, form the mixture into small patties – roughly 8 bite-sized burgers.
3. Heat the oil in a large non-stick pan over a medium-high heat, add the patties and brown for 2 minutes on each side. Don't crowd the pan – cook them in batches if necessary. Transfer to a baking tray then finish cooking them in the oven for 10 minutes.
4. Once the burgers are ready, start assembling. Get your mini skewers – metal or wood – and thread the tomato first, then the lettuce, cheese and lastly the mini burger.

 Tips

- Low-calorie snack

Protein snack option

Pesto Chicken-Stuffed Pittas

SERVES	PREP TIME	COOKING TIME	CALORIES per serving (200g)	CARBS (g)	PROTEIN (g)	FAT (g)	FIBRE (g)
4	5 mins	20 mins	277	21	26	9	4

 Rest Day Recipe

These filled pittas are simply delicious, and of course nutritious. The tasty, antioxidant-packed basil pesto is a perfect partner for the chicken and vegetables. This meal is light on calories and equally light on the tummy, and delivers an excellent protein hit.

INGREDIENTS

1 tbsp olive oil

1 medium onion, chopped

¼ tsp sea salt

400g free range chicken fillets, cut into chunks

1 red pepper, deseeded and sliced

1 yellow pepper, deseeded and sliced

3 tbsp good-quality basil pesto

4 handfuls of baby spinach leaves, washed

4 wholemeal pittas

PREPARATION

1. Heat the olive oil in a pan over a medium heat, add the onion, salt and chicken and fry until the chicken is sealed (about 5 minutes)
2. Add the peppers and stir-fry for about 10 to 12 minutes, until the chicken is cooked through and the peppers are soft. Add the pesto to the pan and mix well with the chicken and peppers, making sure everything is well coated. Cook for another 2 minutes.
3. Lightly toast the pittas, split them open and stuff each with a handful of baby spinach and the warm chicken-pesto mixture.
4. Enjoy!

 Tips

- **A low-calorie meal that will satisfy the taste buds and any hunger cravings**

Provides a great protein hit

Tzatziki Dip with Roast Veggies

SERVES	PREP TIME	COOKING TIME	CALORIES per serving (838g)	CARBS (g)	PROTEIN (g)	FAT (g)	FIBRE (g)
1-2	10 mins	15–20 mins	272	34	25	4.2	15

 Rest Day Recipe

This snack is a healthy choice when matched with nutritious raw or cooked vegetables. Why buy a tzatziki dip when you can whip it up easily at home? You'll be glad you did because it's so fresh and tasty. This snack is light on calories but still really satisfying.

INGREDIENTS

1 red pepper, deseeded and sliced
1 green pepper, deseeded and sliced
a small head of broccoli, florets separated
1 medium carrot, chopped into strips
½ tbsp olive oil
a pinch of sea salt

For the tzatziki:
100g cottage cheese
50g Greek yoghurt
½ a small cucumber, diced
1 tbsp red onion, chopped
1 clove of garlic, peeled and grated
1 tbsp lemon juice
2 tsp fresh dill, chopped
freshly ground black pepper, to taste

PREPARATION

1. Preheat the oven to 180°C.
2. Place the peppers, broccoli and carrot on a baking tray lined with greaseproof paper, drizzle the oil over, sprinkle some salt on top and bake in the oven for 15 minutes.
3. Meanwhile make the tzatziki. Put the cottage cheese, yoghurt, cucumber, red onion, garlic, lemon juice and dill in a bowl and mix well. Season with black pepper.
4. Serve with the oven-roasted veggies.

Tips

- Great as an appetiser or party food
- Low in calories, sugar and saturated fat
- Satisfying snack

SWEET SNACKS AND TREATS

Apple-Berry Oat Crumble

SERVES	PREP TIME	COOKING TIME	CALORIES per serving (241g)	CARBS (g)	PROTEIN (g)	FAT (g)	FIBRE (g)
6	10 mins	60 mins	351	39	7.2	20	7.3

 Exercise Day Recipe

Check out this healthy twist on an apple and berry crumble recipe, made with mixed nuts and ground almonds to give you that extra crunch and texture. Whip up this healthy dessert with a superb blend of fruit and all the classic flavours of an oat crumble. The great thing about it is that it can easily double up as a healthy snack, pre-exercise fuel-up option or even breakfast!

INGREDIENTS

6 medium-sized apples (Pink Lady or Jazz work well), cored and cut into wedges
1 pear, cored and cut into wedges
250ml fresh apple juice
1 tsp vanilla extract
1 tsp ground cinnamon
zest from ½ an orange

For the crumble topping:

100g jumbo porridge oats
100g ground almonds
50g desiccated coconut
1 tsp ground cinnamon
1 tsp vanilla extract
3 tbsp honey
50g mixed nuts
3 tbsp coconut oil
4 tbsp fresh blueberries

PREPARATION

1. Put the apples and pear in a large pot with the apple juice, vanilla, cinnamon and orange zest.
2. Cook over a medium heat for about 30 minutes, stirring occasionally, until the apples have softened.
3. While the fruit is cooking, preheat your oven to 170°C.
4. To make the crumble, put the oats, ground almonds, desiccated coconut, cinnamon, vanilla, honey and nuts in a food processor and blend for a few seconds only (the mix should retain some texture).
5. Melt the coconut oil and stir into the crumble.
6. Pile the cooked apple mixture into a baking dish, spread over the fresh blueberries and scatter the crumble evenly over the top of everything.
7. Bake for 30 minutes or until the crumble is golden.
8. Serve alone or with natural or Greek yoghurt.

Tips

- A moderate calorie-healthy dessert with all the flavour intact
- Almonds offer a good source of healthy fats
- Perfect dessert to bring to a party

Apple Nut Butter Sandwich

SERVES	PREP TIME	CALORIES per serving	CARBS (g)	PROTEIN (g)	FAT (g)	FIBRE (g)
1	2 mins	356	28	9.6	24	8.7

 Rest Day Recipe

This is a great snack that anyone can enjoy but it's a really wonderful way to get children to eat healthy food in a fun way. Apples are a good source of fibre and nutrients, while nut butter provides long-lasting energy, and is a source of protein and healthy fats.

INGREDIENTS

1–2 eating apples, cores removed and cut into large round slices

3 tbsp peanut butter or almond butter

2 tbsp homemade granola (see p. 80)

PREPARATION

1. Spread the nut butter on one side of each apple slice and add a sprinkle of granola.
2. Place another slice of apple on top and press down very gently, to make a 'sandwich'. Continue until you've used up all the ingredients.
3. Enjoy with a glass of milk.

 Tips

- Tasty, crunchy and a good source of healthy fats and fibre
- Really simple and quick to make
- You can cut the apple into all kinds of shapes and sizes to make it more interesting and fun for children to enjoy.

Excellent source of fibre

Battle Bars

MAKES	PREP TIME	SETTING TIME	CALORIES per serving (51g)	CARBS (g)	PROTEIN (g)	FAT (g)	FIBRE (g)
10 bars	15 mins	1 hour	261	13	6.4	21	4.8

 Rest Day Recipe

These bars taste so good you won't believe they are made from nutritious ingredients. They really are a fantastic treat to have if you have worked hard all week and want to indulge yourself with something tasty but still easy to make.

INGREDIENTS

100g almonds, roughly chopped
75g cashew nuts, roughly chopped
50g pistachio nuts, shelled and roughly chopped
3 tbsp raisins
1 tbsp dried cranberries
1 tbsp mixed seeds
20g coconut flakes or desiccated coconut
a pinch of kosher salt
150g dark chocolate (75% cocoa solids)
2 tbsp honey
1 tbsp coconut oil

PREPARATION

1. Put the nuts, raisins, dried cranberries, mixed seeds, coconut and salt into a bowl and mix.
2. In a small saucepan melt the dark chocolate, honey and coconut oil over a low heat.
3. Once the chocolate mix is melted pour it over the mixed chopped nuts and raisins.
4. Pour the mixture into a small rectangular baking tray lined with baking parchment and spread out evenly
5. Put in the fridge for at least an hour and allow to set.
6. Remove from the fridge, turn out onto a chopping board and cut into squares or bars with a sharp knife. Store in an airtight container for up to a week (if you can keep them that long!).

Tips

- **Excellent source of healthy fats**
- **Dark chocolate offers a variety of powerful antioxidants and satisfies a sweet tooth.**

Blueberry Banana Bread

SERVES	PREP TIME	BAKING TIME	CALORIES per serving (106g)	CARBS (g)	PROTEIN (g)	FAT (g)	FIBRE (g)
10	5 mins	75 mins	216	23	10	9.4	2.8

 Rest Day Recipe

There's nothing better than homemade bread. Except blueberry banana homemade bread! Blueberries, banana and natural yoghurt combine well together and help give the bread great texture and flavour. Blueberry banana bread is perfect for a mid-morning snack with a cup of tea or coffee and will provide you with a source of slow-releasing energy.

INGREDIENTS
250g rolled oats
75g mixed nuts and seeds
2 tsp baking powder
a pinch of salt
2 bananas, peeled
3 free range eggs
300g Greek yoghurt
50g fresh blueberries

PREPARATION
1. Preheat oven to 180°C. Grease a 23 x 13cm loaf tin (or line with baking parchment).
2. In a medium-sized bowl, stir the oats, nuts and seeds, baking powder and salt together.
3. In a blender or food processor, blend the bananas and eggs until smooth.
4. Add the wet mix to the oat mixture, add in the yoghurt and stir until just combined and all the oats are well coated.
5. Gently fold in the blueberries with a spoon or spatula, then pour the batter into the prepared tin.
6. Bake for about 70 to 80 minutes, until a toothpick inserted into the centre of the loaf comes out almost dry.
7. Place bread on a wire rack to cool completely before slicing.

Tips

- Gives you a flavour and energy kick to sustain your energy levels for hours
- Great pre-competition fuel-up option when combined with jam or honey
- Blend the oats into a flour before using to give a softer bread with a greater rise.

A delicious mid-morning snack that fits well into any lunch box

Chocolate Protein Squares

MAKES	PREP TIME	SETTING TIME	CALORIES per serving (74g)	CARBS (g)	PROTEIN (g)	FAT (g)	FIBRE (g)
10 squares	10 mins	2 hours	303	23	12	18	4.9

 Rest Day Recipe

These mighty squares are one of my favourite snacks – easy to make and so satisfying. Not only will they manage appetite and a sweet tooth, they are also a good source of protein and slow-releasing carbohydrates from the rolled oats. A word of warning – do not lick the spoon when you blend the nuts, honey and dark chocolate – you will end up with half of the mix gone!

INGREDIENTS

3 large tbsp peanut butter
3 tbsp honey
100g dark chocolate (70% cocoa solids), chopped
50g desiccated coconut
200g oats
100g mixed nuts
2 scoops of chocolate whey protein powder
100ml milk
75g dark chocolate for topping (optional)

PREPARATION

1. First roughly blend the peanut butter, dark chocolate and honey to a coarse mixture, not too smooth.
2. Transfer to a bowl and add the coconut, oats, nuts and protein powder.
3. Mix and add a little milk, then knead all the ingredients together to form a type of dough mixture.
4. Line a 30 x 18cm baking tin with baking parchment and tip the mixture in. Spread it out evenly with clean hands then press down hard to get it all to bind.
5. Put in the fridge to set for about 2 hours.
6. At this stage you can make the squares more indulgent if you like ... melt 75g dark chocolate, spread evenly over the top after 1 hour, then return to the fridge to set completely.
7. Once set, remove and cut into squares with a sharp knife. Store airtight for up to a week.

Tips

- Great mid-morning or mid-afternoon snack with a cup of coffee or tea to fuel your workout
- A practical way to achieve your daily protein target
- Delicious healthy treat
- If you want to reduce the number of calories per portion, simply reduce the portion size by increasing the number of squares you cut at Step 6.

Chocolate Nut Melts

MAKES	PREP TIME	SETTING TIME	CALORIES per serving (49g)	CARBS (g)	PROTEIN (g)	FAT (g)	FIBRE (g)
12	10 mins	1 hour	249	11	8.5	20	2.8

 Rest Day Recipe

The clue for how good this recipe tastes is in the name. With a blend of nuts, seeds and peanut butter folded together in melted chocolate, this is sure to go down as a hit. Keep some leftovers for the lunch box if you can resist eating them all at once.

INGREDIENTS
200g mixed nuts, chopped
30g mixed seeds
3 tbsp dried cranberries or raisins
a pinch of kosher salt
100g dark chocolate (75% cocoa solids)
2 tbsp honey
3 tbsp crunchy peanut butter
1 tbsp coconut oil

PREPARATION
1. Line a 12-cup bun tin with paper cases.
2. Put the chopped nuts, mixed seeds, dried cranberries or raisins and salt in a bowl.
3. In a small saucepan melt the dark chocolate with the honey, peanut butter and coconut oil over a low heat until melted.
4. Pour the chocolate, honey and nut butter mix over the mixed nuts, seeds and fruit and mix well.
5. Using 2 spoons, scrape into baking cases, roughly 1 tbsp each.
6. Put in the fridge for at least an hour and allow to set.
7. Remove from the fridge, serve and gobble. Store airtight for up to a week.

Tips

- Good source of antioxidants in the form of flavonoids from the dark chocolate
- Mixed nuts and seeds provide an excellent source of healthy fats

Great for a mid-morning energy booster

Chocolate Nut Butter Shards

SERVES	PREP TIME	SETTING TIME	CALORIES per serving (63g)	CARBS (g)	PROTEIN (g)	FAT (g)	FIBRE (g)
10	10 mins	1 hour	316	13	7.6	26	6.9

 Rest Day Recipe

This recipe is easy to put together and works well as a party treat for friends. You can break it up and eat it on its own or you can have it with natural yoghurt and fresh blueberries and raspberries as a healthy treat after dinner.

INGREDIENTS

3 tbsp coconut flakes or desiccated coconut
3 tbsp sunflower seeds
3 tbsp pumpkin seeds
3 tbsp sliced almonds
400g dark chocolate (80% cocoa solids)
3 tbsp almond or peanut butter
3 tbsp dried cranberries
a sprinkle of salt

PREPARATION

1. Preheat your oven to 175°C.
2. Spread the coconut, seeds and nuts out on a baking tray and put in the oven for 8 minutes, shaking regularly and watching carefully to prevent burning.
3. Melt the dark chocolate in a Pyrex bowl over a pot of barely simmering hot water. Once melted, mix in the nut butter.
4. Line a baking sheet with a silicone baking mat or parchment paper and spread the chocolate mixture out to an approximate size of 20 x 30cm. While the chocolate is still warm, sprinkle the toasted coconut, nuts and seeds over the chocolate evenly. Finish by scattering the cranberries and a sprinkle of salt.
5. Place in a fridge and chill completely for about an hour until hardened. (Place in a freezer to chill faster if necessary.)
6. Now for the fun bit – peel off the paper and smash into shards of the size you wish.

 Tips

• Simple and quick to whip up for last-minute guests

Source of healthy fats

Cinnamon Bananas

SERVES	PREP TIME	COOKING TIME	CALORIES per serving (164g)	CARBS (g)	PROTEIN (g)	FAT (g)	FIBRE (g)
2	3 mins	10 mins	253	39	7.2	7.5	3.9

 Exercise Day Recipe

This cinnamon banana treat is yummy for two reasons. First the blend of cinnamon, honey and bananas will satisfy your sweet tooth. Second the energy kick from the bananas is perfect to fuel your exercise session or competition.

INGREDIENTS

2 ripe bananas, peeled and sliced lengthways
2 tbsp honey
½ tsp ground cinnamon
2 tbsp flaked almonds
Greek yoghurt, to serve

PREPARATION

1. Preheat your oven to 180°C.
2. Coat the bananas in the honey then sprinkle the cinnamon on top.
3. Place the sliced bananas on a lined baking tray and bake in the oven for 10 minutes.
4. Toast the flaked almonds in the same oven for 4 to 5 minutes or until they begin to turn brown.
5. Remove from the oven and sprinkle the bananas with toasted flaked almonds. Serve warm with Greek or natural yoghurt.

Tips

- Energy booster for a pre-exercise snack
- Great fuel-up snack option
- For an even more indulgent treat, melt some dark chocolate and pour it on top of the bananas and yoghurt.

Only requires 5 simple ingredients

Coconut Date Balls

MAKES	PREP TIME	SETTING TIME	CALORIES per serving (64g)	CARBS (g)	PROTEIN (g)	FAT (g)	FIBRE (g)
8 balls	15 mins	1 hour	255	30	5	13	4.6

 Exercise Day Recipe

The perfect treat to hit your sweet tooth, particularly on an exercise day! Date balls are also an excellent high-energy snack that can be used to top up your energy levels if your training demands are high. The dates need to be soaked for an hour before starting this recipe, so you could do this in advance.

INGREDIENTS

12 medjool dates, pitted
150g raw, unsalted cashew nuts
50g desiccated coconut (plus more for rolling the balls)
freshly grated rind of 1 lemon
juice of ½ a lemon

PREPARATION

1. Soak the dates in warm water for 1 hour.
2. Blend the dates to a pulp with a small amount of water. Add the nuts to the blender and blitz into small pieces.
3. Scrape the date mixture into a large bowl and stir in the coconut, lemon rind and lemon juice until well mixed.
4. Using clean hands, roll the mix into golf ball-sized portions.
5. Roll each ball over a plate covered in desiccated coconut to coat.
6. Refrigerate for 1 hour and serve.

Tips

- Great fuel-up snack option pre-competition
- These balls of energy can keep your energy levels sustained through a demanding day
- Healthy treat

Coconut and Cashew Squares

MAKES	PREP TIME	SETTING TIME	CALORIES per serving (55g)	CARBS (g)	PROTEIN (g)	FAT (g)	FIBRE (g)
10 squares	15 mins	2 hours	255	20	6.7	17	4.7

 Rest Day Recipe

These coconut and cashew squares are an amazing treat or energy-boosting snack for a physically demanding day. They are also a super option for children's lunch boxes instead of a snack bar!

INGREDIENTS

125g jumbo oats

75g coconut flakes or desiccated coconut

150g raw, unsalted cashew nuts, broken and lightly toasted in a dry frying pan

4 tbsp chia seeds

40g dried cranberries, coarsely chopped

4 tbsp honey

3 tbsp peanut butter

2 tbsp coconut oil

¼ tsp salt

½ tsp ground cinnamon

1 tsp vanilla extract

PREPARATION

1. Line a 23cm-square tin with parchment paper.
2. In a large bowl combine the oats, coconut, cashews, chia seeds and dried cranberries.
3. Place a saucepan over a medium heat and put in the honey, peanut butter, coconut oil, salt, cinnamon and vanilla. Stir regularly until the coconut oil is melted with the peanut butter.
4. Add this mixture to the dry ingredients in the bowl and stir well, making sure everything is fully coated.
5. Transfer mixture to the prepared baking tin and, using clean hands, press firmly down to ensure the mixture sticks together – the harder you press, the more they will stick together.
6. Place the tray in the fridge for 2 hours until firm then remove the tray from the fridge.
7. Turn the hardened mixture out onto a large chopping board, peel off the paper and cut into squares using a sharp knife. Store airtight for up to a week.

Tips

- Contains both omega-3 and omega-6 healthy fats

Brilliant lunch box snack or treat

Cottage Cheese Muddle

SERVES	PREP TIME	CALORIES per serving (275g)	CARBS (g)	PROTEIN (g)	FAT (g)	FIBRE (g)
1	5 mins	387	36	19	17	3.9

 Rest Day Recipe

This low-calorie snack is perfect to enjoy in the evening time after training or before bed. Cottage cheese contains slow-releasing protein which will allow you to recover overnight. This snack also works well after an evening training session as the banana provides a source of carbohydrate for recovery.

INGREDIENTS
150g cottage cheese
6 red grapes
2 tsp honey
1 tsp cacao powder
1 tsp crunchy peanut butter
1 tsp flaked almonds
1 small banana, peeled and sliced
1 tbsp fresh raspberries

PREPARATION
1. Place the cottage cheese, grapes, honey and cacao in a blender and whizz together till smooth.
2. Pour into a bowl and top with the peanut butter, flaked almonds, chopped banana and raspberries.

Tips

- Protein-rich evening snack to aid overnight recovery or after evening training session
- Filling snack to satisfy any hunger cravings
- Light on calories

Crunchy Chia Quinoa Bars

MAKES	PREP TIME	COOKING TIME	CALORIES per serving (65g)	CARBS (g)	PROTEIN (g)	FAT (g)	FIBRE (g)
10 bars	10 mins	25 mins	209	22	6.1	11	4.8

 Rest Day Recipe

Quinoa is a wonder grain: it's gluten-free, high in protein and one of the few plant foods that contain all nine essential amino acids. It is also a slow-digesting carbohydrate source that is high in fibre. Quinoa is easy to flavour and is a great option to include in breakfast, lunch or in snack bars like this recipe. The blend of almonds and pecan nuts give these bars a snapping crunch.

INGREDIENTS

100g jumbo oats
75g cup uncooked pre-rinsed quinoa
4 tbsp chia seeds
¼ tsp sea salt
1 tsp ground cinnamon
2 ripe bananas, peeled and mashed
½ tsp vanilla extract
3 tbsp almonds, chopped
3 tbsp pecans, chopped
3 tbsp dried fruit of your choice (e.g. raisins, cranberries)
3 tbsp peanut butter
2 tbsp honey

PREPARATION

1. Preheat your oven to 180°C.
2. Line a 13 x 23cm baking tin with baking parchment.
3. In a large bowl, mix the oats, quinoa, chia seeds, salt and cinnamon, then stir in the banana and vanilla extract. Next add the almonds, pecans and dried fruit and mix again.
4. Place a small saucepan over low heat, add the peanut butter and honey and stir until the mixture is warm and melted into a paste.
5. Pour this paste into the oat mixture and mix everything together until well combined.
6. Pour into the lined pan and press down firmly with clean hands.
7. Bake for 25 minutes or until the edges turn golden brown.
8. Allow to cool before cutting into bars of desired size with a sharp knife. Store in an airtight container for up to a week.

Tips

- Works well as a pre-workout or recovery snack
- Oats, peanut butter and banana provide a great source of stable energy and satisfying fibre

Danger Bars

MAKES	PREP TIME	SETTING TIME	CALORIES per serving (64g)	CARBS (g)	PROTEIN (g)	FAT (g)	FIBRE (g)
15 bars	15 mins	3 hours	175	13	4	11	3.4

 Rest Day Recipe

The danger in these bars comes from wanting more than one once you've tasted them! Have one after a tough day of training or if you want a treat with your cup of tea or coffee. When almond butter, nuts and seeds are combined with honey you get an incredibly tasty and crunchy texture. The calories in the bar come mainly from the nuts and almond butter, which are a good source of healthy fats.

INGREDIENTS
120g almond butter
100g honey
30g coconut oil
120g oats
70g mixed seeds
60g raw cocoa nibs
30g chia seeds

PREPARATION
1. In medium-sized pan on a medium heat, melt the almond butter, honey and coconut oil. Do not boil or allow the mixture to caramelise.
2. Remove from the heat, quickly add the remaining dry ingredients and mix well.
3. Spread the mix in a shallow 20 x 20cm tin, lined with baking parchment.
4. Refrigerate for at least 3 hours.
5. Remove from the tin, turn onto a board, peel off the paper and cut into 15 bars.

 Tips

- **Excellent source of healthy fats**

Treat or snack recipe

Dark Chocolate Bounty Balls

MAKES	PREP TIME	CALORIES per serving (54g)	CARBS (g)	PROTEIN (g)	FAT (g)	FIBRE (g)
8 balls	15 mins	265	7.1	3.9	23	5.6

 Rest Day Recipe

Coconut and dark chocolate are a match made in heaven. These two go hand and hand and complement each other perfectly when the sweet taste of coconut is held together by a dark chocolate coating. Delectable with your cup of coffee.

INGREDIENTS

2 tbsp coconut oil
150 g desiccated coconut
3 tbsp coconut cream
2 tbsp Greek yoghurt
1 tbsp honey
100g dark chocolate (I use Lindt 90% cocoa solids)

PREPARATION

1. Melt the coconut oil in a saucepan on a low heat.
2. Mix the desiccated coconut, coconut cream, yoghurt and honey in a medium-sized bowl.
3. With clean hands, roll the mixture into small balls and place on a plate covered with a sheet of greaseproof paper.
4. Melt the chocolate in a Pyrex bowl set over a saucepan of barely simmering water, then, using your fingers and a spoon, roll the balls in the melted chocolate until completely covered. Return to the plate and leave to harden in the fridge.

Tips

- A ball of sweetness, wrapped in melted dark chocolate
- Calories are quite high so exercise portion control!
- Low-carb snack option
- Be patient when rolling the balls for the best possible outcome!

Mixed Berry Recovery Smoothie

SERVES	PREP TIME	CALORIES per serving (447g)	CARBS (g)	PROTEIN (g)	FAT (g)	FIBRE (g)
1	2 mins	534	76	30	15	12

  Exercise Day Recipe

This is an ideal smoothie option after an intense workout. It is a good source of carbohydrate and is high in protein and essential nutrients needed to repair damaged muscles. On top of all those benefits, it's easy to make and really tasty!

INGREDIENTS

200ml almond or whole milk
1 scoop of vanilla whey protein powder (or 2 tbsp low-fat Greek yoghurt)
10 grapes, mixed red and green
3 large strawberries, hulled
3 tbsp blueberries
1 tbsp raspberries
1 banana, peeled
1 tbsp honey
1 tbsp almond butter
2 ice cubes

PREPARATION

1. Whizz all the ingredients together in a blender and serve. Adjust the amount of milk if necessary – use less if you want a thicker smoothie you can eat with a spoon.

Tips

- **Protein and carbohydrate for muscle recovery**
- **Balanced and nutritious smoothie with a good source of fibre**

Dark Chocolate Super Smoothie

SERVES	PREP TIME	COOKING TIME	CALORIES per serving (437g)	CARBS (g)	PROTEIN (g)	FAT (g)	FIBRE (g)
1	2 mins	2 mins	481	34	36	23	5.4

 Rest Day Recipe

What's so super about a dark chocolate smoothie, you ask. Well, it tastes delicious but still provides an excellent protein hit and is a good source of carbohydrate. It's also not too high in calories but still satisfies your hunger while providing an abundance of nutrients. Enjoy as a perfectly healthy, guilt-free snack and alter the combination of ingredients to suit your energy needs. This smoothie rocks.

INGREDIENTS
150ml almond or whole milk (or water if you want to reduce the calorie content)
1 scoop of chocolate protein powder – whey, hemp or pea protein
1 banana, peeled
1 square of dark chocolate (85% cocoa solids)
2 tbsp Greek yoghurt
1 tbsp almond butter
1 tsp manuka honey
3 ice cubes

PREPARATION
1. Blend all the ingredients and serve with a little grated dark chocolate on top.

 Tips

- Has a 1:1 blend of carbohydrates and proteins to fuel or recover from a workout
- A great way to hit your protein needs
- Turn this into a breakfast smoothie by simply adding 2 tbsp porridge oats before blending

Rich source of antioxidants

Fruit and Nut Protein Bars

MAKES	PREP TIME	SETTING TIME	CALORIES per serving (69g)	CARBS (g)	PROTEIN (g)	FAT (g)	FIBRE (g)
10 bars	10 mins	2 hours	257	23	13	13	3.3

 Rest Day Recipe

These bars are quick and easy to make and come in handy for a nutritious snack on the go. Pack them in the car or in your lunch box for a snack option in school, college or work. I often chop these into smaller pieces and to enjoy with my tea after dinner as a healthy treat.

INGREDIENTS

200g oats
3 scoops of chocolate whey protein powder
75g mixed seeds (e.g. pumpkin, sesame, sunflower)
100g mixed nuts and dried fruits (easily sourced ready-mixed in supermarkets)
1 tbsp honey
100ml milk of choice
100g dark chocolate (75% cocoa solids), broken into pieces

PREPARATION

1. Put all the dry ingredients into a bowl and mix together.
2. Add the honey and milk and knead everything together with clean hands to form a dough-like mixture.
3. Tip the mixture into a baking tray lined with baking parchment and spread evenly. Press down hard to get it all to bind.
4. Put the tray in the fridge to set for 2 hours.
5. Once set cut into bars using a sharp knife.

Tips

- Excellent recovery snack option
- Store in your gym bag for a snack after an intense training session
- You could use disposable plastic gloves to mix the ingredients together to avoid getting your hands sticky.
- Add the milk very slowly. Too much milk and the bars get way too moist and sticky!

Mini Toasted Chocolate Nut Clusters

MAKES	PREP TIME	COOKING TIME	CALORIES per serving (44g)	CARBS (g)	PROTEIN (g)	FAT (g)	FIBRE (g)
8 clusters	10 mins	12 mins	231	11	5.6	18	3.2

 Rest Day Recipe

These are a great idea for a Sunday treat with tea or coffee, or for children's parties. Nut clusters also work great with added dried fruit like raisins and dried cranberries – just stir them in at Step 4.

INGREDIENTS
50g cashew halves

50g whole almonds

50g hazelnuts

50g walnuts, crushed slightly in your hands

3 tbsp raw honey

1 tbsp agave syrup

1 tsp vanilla extract

75g dark chocolate (70% cocoa solids), broken into chunks

PREPARATION
1. Preheat the oven to 200°C. Line a muffin tin with 8 muffin cases.
2. Put all the nuts in a large bowl and mix to combine.
3. In a separate bowl, mix the honey with the agave syrup and vanilla extract.
4. Pour your wet ingredient mixture over the top of your dry ingredients and mix them together until all the nuts are evenly coated.
5. Carefully spoon the mixture into the cases, using two spoons if that makes it easier.
6. Place your nut clusters in the oven and cook for 10 to 12 minutes, or until the tops are lightly golden.
7. Remove from the oven and allow to cool for 5 minutes before carefully transferring to a wire rack to cool.
8. Last, melt the dark chocolate in a Pyrex bowl set over a saucepan of barely simmering water and spoon over the nut clusters, allowing them to set before serving.

 Tips

- **Excellent source of healthy fats**

Nut Butter Protein Brownies

MAKES	PREP TIME	COOKING TIME	CALORIES per serving (81g)	CARBS (g)	PROTEIN (g)	FAT (g)	FIBRE (g)
10 brownies	10 mins	20 mins	290	8.5	15	22	3.2

 Rest Day Recipe

These nut butter protein brownies go well with every occasion and that's just because they taste so good. Packed into the brownies are avocado, eggs and peanut butter. These give these brownies flavour and keep them moist. Great at any time, but perfect with a mid-morning cup of coffee.

INGREDIENTS
120g dark chocolate (85% cocoa solids)
120g peanut butter
40g coconut oil
4 free range eggs
2 tbsp dark honey
3 scoops casein / whey protein powder (chocolate or vanilla flavour)
1 ripe avocado, puréed
2 tbsp flaked almonds

PREPARATION
1. Preheat the oven to 175°C. Line a baking tin with greaseproof paper.
2. Melt the chocolate, nut butter and coconut oil together in a Pyrex bowl set over a saucepan of gently simmering water.
3. Remove from the heat, add the eggs and honey and beat into a thick mixture.
4. Add the protein powder and mix well. When the powder is fully combined, add in the avocado and mix through until it's also fully combined. Finally, mix through the flaked almonds.
5. Carefully pour into the baking tin and bake for 20 minutes.

 Tips

- Great for any occasion, especially after a workout for a protein hit
- Eggs are a complete source of protein and contain all your required amino acids
- Avocados and nuts are a good source of healthy fat

Nut-Berry Protein Snack Pot

SERVES	PREP TIME	CALORIES per serving (120g)	CARBS (g)	PROTEIN (g)	FAT (g)	FIBRE (g)
1	2 mins	344	16	23	21	6.8

 Rest Day Recipe

This snack has it all – protein, slow-releasing carbs and the combination of nuts, seeds and Greek yoghurt offers a variety of healthy fats. All of this adds up to a great recovery recipe. Make it ahead to enjoy later, or devour immediately.

INGREDIENTS
3 tbsp oats
1 tbsp chia seeds
1 tbsp pecan nuts, roughly chopped
1 tbsp desiccated coconut
1 tbsp milled hemp or vanilla whey protein
2 tbsp Greek yoghurt

For the topping:
1 tbsp fresh blueberries
1 tbsp fresh raspberries
1 tbsp flaked almonds
1 tbsp pumpkin seeds
1 tsp dark chocolate (85% cocoa solids), grated

PREPARATION
1. In a small bowl, mix the oats, chia seeds, pecan nuts, desiccated coconut, hemp or whey and Greek yoghurt.
2. Pour the mix into a pot (if eating immediately) or jar with a lid (if eating later).
3. Top with the blueberries, raspberries, flaked almonds, pumpkin seeds and grated dark chocolate. Pop the lid on the jar and refrigerate if you're going to eat it later.

 Tips

- **High-protein snack**

Ideal to snack on late in the evening

Protein Booster Bars

MAKES	PREP TIME	SETTING TIME	CALORIES per serving (62g)	CARBS (g)	PROTEIN (g)	FAT (g)	FIBRE (g)
8 bars	12 mins	2 hours	249	14	17	14	4

 Rest Day Recipe

There is currently an abundance of protein bars on the market that you could buy but what about making your own? That way you know exactly what you are eating, and you avoid all the processed ingredients!

INGREDIENTS

60g porridge oats or oat
  flour
5 (25g) scoops of whey,
  hemp or protein powder,
  chocolate or vanilla
  flavour
3 tbsp ground almonds
3 tbsp mixed seeds
  (e.g. pumpkin, sesame,
  sunflower)
3 tbsp dark chocolate chips
1 tbsp desiccated coconut
2 tbsp chia seeds
2 tbsp honey
4 tbsp peanut butter
50–100ml milk of choice

PREPARATION

1. Put all the dry ingredients (the first 7) in a large bowl and mix well.
2. Add the honey and peanut butter and mix well.
3. Add the milk in small amounts until the mix comes together to form a thick paste. Don't add too much milk at once, you don't want the mixture to be too wet or sticky.
4. Line a 13 x 23cm baking tin with baking parchment and add the mixture. Spread the mixture out evenly with clean hands, then press down firmly.
5. Cover the tray and place in the fridge for 2 hours.
6. Remove from the fridge and use a sharp knife to cut into 8 bars.
7. Store the bars in an airtight container to keep them fresh. It's a good idea to wrap each bar individually in greaseproof paper when storing to stop them sticking together.

Tips

• Great for a lunch box or recovery snack
• Great source of protein – the name says it all!

Seán's Pre-Match Creamed Rice

SERVES	PREP TIME	COOKING TIME	CALORIES per serving (393g)	CARBS (g)	PROTEIN (g)	FAT (g)	FIBRE (g)
3	5 mins	40 mins	400	84	12	2.5	1.3

 Exercise Day Recipe

Most athletes think a pre-competition meal has to be something like rice or pasta with chicken; it certainly doesn't have to be. The aim of a pre-competition meal is to simply top up fuel stores, so it can be any decent small or medium-sized meal. Athletes love routine and Seán O'Brien is no different. His favourite pre-match meal is this delicious creamed rice recipe. It has worked perfectly to keep the Tullow tank fuelled up and ready to perform at his best when playing an intense 80 minutes of rugby.

INGREDIENTS
150g pudding or arborio rice
600ml low-fat milk or almond milk
200ml water
2 tbsp honey or maple syrup

Toppings:
a handful of fresh blueberries
1 ripe banana, peeled and sliced
½ tsp ground cinnamon
1 tbsp honey or maple syrup
sliced peaches or mango (optional)

PREPARATION
1. Place the rice, milk, water, maple syrup or honey in a large non-stick saucepan. Give it a good stir, then place the pan on a very low heat.
2. Cook gently for around 40 minutes, or until thick and creamy, stirring regularly.
3. Loosen the rice pudding with some extra milk before serving, but only if needed.
4. Remove from the heat, allow to cool a little, then serve the rice pudding with the blueberries and banana, cinnamon and maple syrup or honey drizzled on top. Add peach or mango if desired.

Tips

- Perfect pre-competition top-up meal
- Low in fibre and easy to digest
- High in carbohydrate

GLOSSARY

CARB LOADING	Carbohydrate loading is a strategy used by athletes, such as runners or elite team sport athletes, to maximise the storage of glycogen (energy) in the muscles and liver. The strategy is to eat high-carbohydrate meals in the 36 hours before exercise competition.
FUEL-UP	This refers to a meal that contains a high proportion of carbohydrate to fuel exercise.
HEALTHY FATS	Healthy fats are polyunsaturated and monounsaturated fats (omega-3 and omega-6 essential fatty acids) that are beneficial to your health when eaten in the correct proportions.
HIGH ENERGY	When referring to a meal, this means that it is high in calories, but not necessarily high in carbohydrate, so there is a key difference. A high-carbohydrate meal is more appropriate where there is a significant cost of energy resulting from high-intensity exercise (see page 53).
HIGH-INTENSITY EXERCISE	High-intensity exercise means short-term training under stress for 30–60 minutes. When doing this type of exercise, your heart rate is above 140 beats per minute, you are sweating profusely, breathing heavily and talking is hard!
LOW-INTENSITY ACTIVITY	Activity that does not require effort or does not result in significant energy expenditure.
MIXED MEAL	A meal that combines a balance of protein, carbohydrates and fats that results in a slow release of energy into your body.

POST	After exercise/training/workout
PRE	Before exercise/training/workout
PROTEIN HIT	A meal that provides approximately 20g of protein, helping you achieve your total protein intake.
RECOVERY	A meal that contains optimum amounts of protein and carbohydrate foods to replace depleted energy levels and facilitate muscle repair.
WORKOUT/ TRAINING	A workout or training doesn't have to be gym- or field-based; it can be any form of exercise or manual labour that raises your heart rate, fatigues your muscles and results in you burning calories.

REFERENCES

The nutrition analysis in this book was completed using 'Nutritics', the nutrition management software. See www.nutritics.com

Aune, D., Giovannucci, E., Boffetta, P., Fadnes, L.T., Keum, N., Norat, T., Greenwood, D.C., Riboli, E., Vatten, L.J. and Tonstad, S., 2017. Fruit and vegetable intake and the risk of cardiovascular disease, total cancer and all-cause mortality—a systematic review and dose-response meta-analysis of prospective studies. *International Journal of Epidemiology*, 46(3), pp. 1029–1056.

Impey, S.G., Hearris, M.A., Hammond, K.M., Bartlett, J.D., Louis, J., Close, G.L. and Morton, J.P., 2018. Fuel for the work required: A theoretical framework for carbohydrate periodisation and the glycogen threshold hypothesis. *Sports Medicine*, 48(5), pp. 1031–1048.

Maughan, R.J., Burke, L.M., Dvorak, J., Larson-Meyer, D.E., Peeling, P., Phillips, S.M., Rawson, E.S., Walsh, N.P., Garthe, I., Geyer, H. and Meeusen, R., 2018. IOC consensus statement: dietary supplements and the high-performance athlete. *International Journal of Sport Nutrition and Exercise Metabolism*, 28(2), pp. 104-125.

National Adult Nutrition Survey, Summary Report on Food and Nutrient Intakes, Physical Measurements, Physical Activity Patterns and Food Choice Motives. Irish Universities Nutrition Alliance. Edited by Dr Janette Walton.

Rodriguez, N.R., Di, N.M. and Langley, S., 2009. American College of Sports Medicine position stand. Nutrition and athletic performance. *Medicine and Science in Sports and Exercise*, 41(3), pp. 709–731.

Reynolds, A., Mann, J., Cummings, J., Winter, N., Mete, E. and Te Morenga, L., 2019. Carbohydrate quality and human health: a series of systematic reviews and meta-analyses. *The Lancet*.

INDEX

D